Come To Life

Some of the revelations in this book might just offend you momentarily, but you are asked to continually read with an opened mind and you will learn to make a clear distinction between what is true and what is obviously a lie!

If the good people of this world are going to survive an uncertain and possibly a dreadful future, the good people of this earth must unite, have grim reaper's funeral and bury him or her once and for all!

Come To Life

DJWA

Come To Life...
AND LIVE FOREVER IN THE FLESH!

©

THE LIBRARY OF CONGRESS
COPYRIGHT OFFICE

101 Independence Ave., S. E.
Washington, D. C. 20559 – 6000

TXn 909 – 750
24 JUN 1999

International Standard Book Number 0-9705265-1-2

DJWA

ISBN : 0-9705265-1-2

To Order additional copies, please contact us.

BookSurge, LLC
www.booksurge.com
1-866-308-6235
orders@booksurge.com

Come To Life

TABLE OF CONTENTS

ACKNOWLEDGEMENTS

No professional author, nor any serious writer on any level, should ever copy another writer's ideas or labor, without giving that writer appropriate credit, be that one word; one sentence; one paragraph; one page or whatever. Although the Bible and other famous Holy Books are all quote-worthy, there has never been a book as complete as the one you are about to read. Furthermore, no other single book, nor any other three rolled into one, is as informative or can suggest that this book has been copied from it or them. However, many books have been read that led to the writing of this book, and many books have been used to support this book's premise. (e.g., grim reaper's picture: courtesy of Microsoft Internet Explorer @ yahoo.com). As many sources as were remembered are listed in this book's body or its bibliography. Nonetheless, books written by communities like the Abelard Reuchlin Foundation (those who hold the key to the escape-door leading from the classical mess); great models like Grand Master Albert Pike (a builder of men); a little man who started out as Mr. Elijah Poole (who freed millions of his people from the grave of mental slavery); and great books like the Holy Bible, Holy Qur'an, Bhagavad Gita, Sacred Scriptures, Book of Jasher, Sacred Books of the East, and the Lost Books of the Bible and the Hidden Books of Eden, all must be given the highest praises possible. Many doctrines and many hard-working individuals have assumed vital roles in attempting to bring immortality to you many years before this book was conceived. The contents of this book give special tribute to as many of those hard-working individuals as were remembered!

PREFACE

Because of the delicate nature of this book, no college or university names will be mentioned. However, the credentials of Djwa are impeccable, well documented and can be confirmed. The author has been employed as a university librarian for nineteen years and has completed over four hundred academic hours at reputable colleges and universities. In college, thirty hours per year is considered full-time enrollment. Three hundred hours, alone, is equivalent to ten consecutive years of full-time enrollment, non-stop. The author has two associate degrees and a bachelor's degree with a triple minor. The author has completed three (3) master's degrees from very reputable universities. He has also completed all of his doctoral course work in Higher Education on the doctoral level.

This book is intended, through a series of short essays, parables, common sense analogies, short stories, and short recollections of very relevant incidents in the author's life to make this book totally non-lacking. This book provides any serious reader interested in ancient beliefs, in understanding humanitarianism, and in understanding world religions with the following: (1) liberation from confusion and enslavement caused by established beliefs and misinterpretation of holy and/or sacred scriptures; (2) liberation from the guilt of loving oneself; (3) courage to believe in what is actually written; and (4) liberation from death and the fear of dying.

Ironically, after traveling throughout the world, examining other cultures, and seeing that every different nation had a prophet, God, and/or messiah that looked just like the indigenous people of the land, the author became puzzled. The idea of all cultures having their own prophets, messiahs, and saviors, led the author on a desperate search for truth, and ultimately, total liberation from the classical mess.

It was discovered that language and religion is the epitome of one's culture, if not one's culture in its entirety. Thus, this book was written. This book was organized, primarily, to contribute, as much as possible, to one's pursuit of knowledge; especially, if that pursuit of knowledge includes unbiased learning. Restricted only by its size and number of pages, this book teaches as much hidden knowledge about all established religions and doctrines as possible, and it teaches as much common sense as possible. It teaches one to distinguish between belief and history; it offers a simple route to immortality; and it extends a diet to help make this mission complete.

The author began studying foreign languages, cultures, and beliefs in 1967. He traveled throughout the United States, Mexico, Hawaii, Philippines, Japan, Okinawa, and Asia and studied Buddhism in Southeast Asia. He lived in Thailand and learned the language of the Thai people. He studied a form of martial arts known as Tae kwon do, under Master Suk Jhoon Ahn of Korea. The author once taught Tae kwon do in the Korean Language. He has studied the Holy Bible (King James Version, as well as many others). He has studied the Bhagavad Gita (Upanishads and the Vedas); the Book of The Dead; the Holy Qur'an and the Koran. He has studied the Sacred Scriptures of the East and understands the Eight-Fold Path and the Four

Noble Truths (Buddhism). He has studied the Apocrypha (Catholicism); and, of course, many other less powerful doctrines. Why must an individual worship messengers, prophets, and gods who others tell them to worship? The author wanted to know why it is considered deviant behavior, when an individual decides to be different. Thus, this book was written!

Concerning religion, the author finds it very easy to believe that which is written in the Holy Books of all nations and can easily relate to the Christian, Buddhist, Muslim, Judaist, Hindu, Taoist, of course the Coptic, and all other established faiths. However, the author finds it completely ironic and totally baffling that, although each religious book teaches the very same righteous concept, mysteriously, each book seems to be misunderstood or misinterpreted (almost as if purposely) in the exact same manner. It makes one wonder whether this misinterpretation is a devious plan, by the rich and powerful minority of all nations, to maintain total control of the masses of all races and keep them poor and ignorant, while they alone remain rich and aware of what is going on in the world.

This book attempts to make clear the distinction between what Christians teach and what the Bible really says. It teaches what Muhammad actually did and what Muhammad tried to do. It teaches of the errors of the world that caused Buddha to leave a beautiful wife, a son, and a life of wealth and riches, for a lonely life of six long years of fasting and submission to poverty, and, of course, much more.

The author also expounds briefly on the religious beliefs of the Jewish people, Islam, Hinduism, and other religions of the East and the West. Therefore, the reader is asked to read carefully with an open mind and without the fear of disappointing other people who care very little about the reader, or themselves. Brothers and sisters (black, brown, red, yellow, and white), this book was written for your enjoyment as well as for your enlightenment. So, you are asked to enjoy this little book, because, indeed, you will learn more about things you have never even heard before than you ever thought possible? Also, after reading this book, the reader will know more in-depth knowledge about religion and its major prophets than most preachers and ministers who preside over churches and congregations. Moreover, and the most amazing thing; dying after reading this book is entirely up to the reader!

This book is dedicated to every single individual on this earth (man and woman) who wants peace, immortality, good health, beauty, riches, and good will to him and herself and to all of his and her man and womankind.

THE HOLY BIBLE

WHAT DO
SCRIPTURES REALLY SAY?

Most adults can look back on their early childhood years and remember being told things they know today, after they have grown wiser, that are simply not true. Many adults remember being told about the "Tooth Fairy"! They also remember being warned about good old Santa Claus. Some can even remember when they decided to pretend to be asleep one Christmas Eve and catch Santa Claus bringing their presents. However, when they peeked in, they saw their father and their mother trying desperately to set things up, before they awoke the next morning. They may have been a little disappointed at first, but as they grew older and thought about it, they felt liberated. Did you not as well? They could now tell younger children, who they knew, that there was no Santa Claus." Some might even remember that it may have felt good being an older kid and now being able to burst the smaller kids' tiny little bubbles.

Finally, after becoming adults themselves, though, many probably have overheard their kids arguing, and probably have heard the younger kids putting up a fight to defend the existence of good old Santa Claus. Even as children, people learn not to want to let go of something that makes them feel good. So, when someone attempts to take that something away, whether it is tangible, intangible, animate, inanimate, or whatever the case may be, people resist.

However, many people realize that one does not have to be a kid, to have his or her bubble burst. Most children as they mature, find themselves learning something amazing and new, every year of their life, and usually find themselves parting from a separate set of lies each one of those years. Finally, though, when even the earliest adulthood is reached, people should then be more than ready to let go of any and all lies! Should they not? Are you an adult? Are you ready?

When a new car is purchased, an owner's manual comes with it telling the owner what type of fuel to use, how much air to put in the tires, and how often to get oil changes, among other requirements. Is this correct? Remember though, the owner's manual does not make the owner follow these requirements; besides, the car belongs to the owner, and the owner can do whatever he or she wants with his or her car. Is this correct?

Likewise, many believe the bible and other holy books are like owner's manuals for the human body. Remember, in the Christian bible, God in Genesis 1:29-30 tells humans and animals what they were meant to eat. Again, remember though, God did not say that humans and animals could not eat anything else except vegetables; although, it is more than obvious that vegetables were the only foods given to be eaten in these verses; besides, with teeth sharp enough, a fool knows that just about anything can be eaten, but the results (sickness and death) just might not be the most desirable results. Is this correct?

Remember, when God gives a commandment in the Bible or in any other holy book, God does not say, "You most definitely cannot," God says "do not." There is a difference; in the latter, one is given freedom of choice. When one buys an automobile and attempts to put fuel in his or her automobile, one might discover a small printed warning label or stamp indicating "unleaded fuel only." The warning does not say "you cannot pump or pour anything but unleaded fuel in this hole." Does it? Now, remember, it is that person's car, and that person can put any kind of fuel he or she wants to put in his or her own car; therefore, the manufacturer warns the owner to use "unleaded fuel only." Similarly, God, apparently, is the manufacturer of man, and in Genesis 1:29, God tells man, "I have given you every herb bearing seed, and to you it shall be for meat."

What does this mean? Does one have to possess some kind of extraordinary supernatural insight, or have someone perform some type of major translating or interpreting for them to understand something that seems so obvious and so "point blank?"

Is the Bible being purposely misinterpreted by the preachers and ministers of today, or can they just simply not read very well? For example, how many animals did Noah place on the Ark? Were there two of every kind? No! That is not what the King James Version of the Holy Bible says!

In Genesis 7:1-2, it reads that there were seven pairs of every clean beast and two pairs of every unclean beast. Have the preachers been lying all these years or just plain ignorant? Has there been a distinction made between the clean and the unclean beast, since the beginning of time? Were different animals created to serve different purposes? Does the Bible lie, or do the many so-called interpreters of the Bible lie, whether knowingly or unknowingly? Yes, it is pretty easy to guess where the lie or the very critical misinterpretation is coming from, and this is why it is so important for an individual to read his or her holy book for him or herself. Can people really trust another fallible individual to read something for them that they depend upon for the salvation of their soul?

Of all the thousands of preachers and ministers, it seems as though, at least, one of them should have read Genesis, chapter seven, verses one and two. What are they afraid of? Are they too weak to believe in and follow what is written? Is the reader? How many times has the reader witnessed a Christian, black and/or white, say to a Muslim or Jew, "oh, you don't eat pork, do you? Many times, huh?

They say this, as though God has exempted them from something that he has required of others. Then, when they are shown in the Bible, in Leviticus 11:7-8 and in Deuteronomy 14:8, where they have been commanded not to eat pork just as Jews and Muslims, they say, "that's in the Old Testament," as though God has changed his mind about what is clean or unclean. Well, maybe some of these good people are not reading the New Testament either.

In the New Testament, in the book of Matthew, 5:17-18, Jesus said, out of his own mouth that he did not come to destroy the law, and that the law would not change, until heaven and earth has passed away, not until all has been fulfilled. Has heaven and earth passed away? Has all, meaning every single prophecy, been fulfilled?

Some, obviously, wantonly contrary individuals, brothers and sisters wanting to hold on to those pickled pig-feet and those smothered chitterlings (swine intestines), will say, "Jesus is the fulfillment of the law". Yes, maybe so, but this is not being disputed. Matthew 5:18 says that the law will remain the same, until heaven and earth has passed away, until all has been fulfilled! Has heaven (and earth) really passed away? The earth is gone, and people are really just walking around in thin air, imagining they are walking around on earth, imagining all this stuff is still here, huh? Yes, the earth is obviously still here, or everything else would be gone, as well!

If all has been fulfilled, then why are so many loyal believers still waiting on the return of Jesus? Why are so many people waiting for all of those things to happen that are written in the book of Revelation? Has Jesus returned? Have the "Seven Seals" been broken? Has "New Jerusalem" been built? Many things have not been fulfilled, according to the beliefs of many? Verse eighteen says, "Until all has been fulfilled, and it says, "until heaven and earth has passed", not one jot (letter) or one tittle (stroke) will pass from the law. Is there someone else, in the New Testament, who knows more than Jesus, about the law? Who knows more about God's law than Jesus?

Jesus was a Jew, right? What is a Jew, a person from Jewville or Jewland? No! A Jew is a person who believes in the Almighty Lord Jehovah and one who follows the Torah or the Old Testament. Some Arabs eat pork, but no Muslim eats pork, because at the moment he or she is eating pork, Islam requiring that Muslims must not eat pork, this person is obviously not a Muslim. After the pork has been devoured and digested, though, a person can return to being a Muslim, the Muslim God, Allah, being all-forgiving.

A person can be an Arab and not necessarily be a Muslim? Are all Americans Christians? Are all Indians Hindu? No, of course not! The point is that Jesus was a Jew because of his belief not because of his race! One can be an Israelite, or even a member of the Tribe of Judah, and not be a Jew. So, the true Jew, or the true follower of the Jewish faith, does not eat pork. Many Jews don't even eat meat and cheese together. Their religion does not allow them to consume milk and meat together.

At a new McDonald's restaurant, when first opened in Israel, it was forbidden to serve a "Milkshake" with a "BigMac." The point is, if someone says they are following Jesus, and they make it a point to eat pig feet, pigtails, and chitterlings, every chance they get, they need to check themselves; they might just be following someone else. They might not be following Jesus!

In the book of Leviticus, in the eleventh chapter, in the last four verses, God tells you to be holy, and to make a distinction between the beasts that may be eaten and the ones that may not be eaten. Leviticus 11:7 and Deuteronomy 14:8 tell you not to eat the hog, and in Isaiah 66:17, it tells you that anyone eating the hog, when the Lord comes, shall all be killed. Remember Matthew 5:17-19. Don't ask anyone else what they think! Read it for yourself!

Many sinners will put up a horrible fight, when you try to snatch those smoked sausages and smothered chitterlings out of his or her mouth, and say, "it's not what goes into the mouth that defiles the man, but it's what comes out of the mouth that defiles the man, because it comes from the heart". Yes, this is true, if this discussion was about the man and not the body. Let us not confuse the two? Hitler, was a vegetarian, he did not drink or smoke, but many would consider him a defiled man; although, Hitler's body was quite clean. Mass murder and the torturing of human beings is the worst of all sins and crimes! However, eating pork will not make you a bad person, it will simply contaminate your body to sickness, possibly to surgery, but, most assuredly, eventually to death!

Some will growl over those pig ears and pig feet, when one attempts to kick the swine's flesh from in front of them and say, "God told Peter to rise and slay and eat, and that everything he made was clean!" This is the biggest and most misleading of all the lies that individuals use to justify the eating of the hog and other divinely forbidden animals! Read Acts 10:15, in the fifteenth verse it specifically says, "What God has cleansed," that is what one is not supposed to call common or unclean, it never says, once, that believers can now eat unclean animals, and that an individual cannot call unclean things unclean!

Don't be deceived by people who are afraid to see clean believers, or by people who fear the unity which might develop between believers and God once believers become clean? Notice how proud a mother is of her children, when they are clean, and how she hides them from the world, when they are not. How much more proud of God's people would God be, once God's people are as clean as God wants them to be (inside and out)?

Finally, not like in the book of 1 Timothy 4:3, in verse three, people are not asked to abstain from those meats which God has created to be received, people are only being asked to read the Bible for themselves and to abstain from those meats which God did not create to be received. Furthermore, first Timothy four, in the fourth verse, it says that every creature (of God) is good, but it does not say that every creature is good. Read it without the Phrase (of God)? This is what people are being told the Bible says, and it does not!

Moreover, hypocrites should stop mocking believers for not eating pork. Believers are merely guilty of believing what they read, and simply do not have time to go through all of that hypocritical irony, every time they meet others who either do not read or who do not believe what they read!

THE ORIGIN OF

THE SEASON CALLED
CHRISTMAS

According to a more-than-five-thousand-year-old Egyptian myth, a very lovable and trustworthy man called Osiris was born to Nut: the vault of the heavens which devours the sun at evening and gives it birth at morning, Osiris' mother, and to Geb: the earth which suggests strong fertility, his father. Seth, Isis, and Nephthys were also children of Nut and Geb. Seth was married to Nephthys, and Osiris married Isis.

Osiris was placed on the throne as King over all Egypt. Osiris brought civilization to Egypt by returning his people, who in many regions had become almost cannibalistic, back to vegetarianism, and teaching them scientific means of agriculture, how to worship the Gods of the heavens, and the laws of the universe and their meanings.

After civilizing Egypt, Osiris began to spread his goodness to neighboring countries, and while away, left his wife, Isis, to rule Egypt in his absence. Seth, the brother of Osiris, also known as Typhon, became very envious of his brother, having never experienced sitting on the throne over Egypt; thus, he plotted against Isis's rule and eventually against his brother's life.

Once when Osiris had been traveling abroad and was due to return soon, Seth planned a huge festival, supposedly for the return of Osiris. Typhon plotted to capture Osiris, by constructing a beautiful box which would only fit Osiris's body. Seth told everyone present at the festival that the one who fit the box most perfectly could have it for his or her very own.

When Osiris got into the box, Seth and his co-conspirators quickly closed the box and rushed away with it, later casting it into the Nile River. The box containing Osiris's body was found by Isis and revived. Osiris is known, through Egyptian writings, to have taken the throne for a second time. Seth, now, was even more evil and more determined than before to get rid of Osiris, and this time, Seth plotted more viciously. Seth and his co-conspirators openly attacked Osiris, while he was alone, and murdered him.

After Osiris was dead, Seth had his body cut into fourteen pieces and distributed to fourteen different places far apart from each other. Nevertheless, Isis found every piece but one. His phallus, suspected to have been eaten by fishes due to being thrown into the Nile, could not be found, but from memory, Isis had his phallus constructed out of the finest gold. However, upon trying to resurrect Osiris a second time, Isis discovered that it could not be done, because part of his body was not human, and he had to be resurrected to the underworld.

One night though, Osiris visited Isis in the form of a spirit, and she conceived and became pregnant. Isis, though, gave birth to their son in the wilderness of the Nile Delta, attempting to escape the pursuing Seth who was trying desperately to kill her and the unborn child, Horus. Isis appealed to Ra while on the run and, and through his intervention, Isis and Horus were saved. Isis learned many of Ra's secrets, taught them to the young warrior Horus, and he became a mighty warrior and eventually defeated and killed Seth, his evil uncle.

To make a long story short, when Horus became an adult, he mysteriously had changed back into Osiris; afterwards, he married Isis, the woman who had bore him, who was once also his wife, and afterwards also, before his death, Osiris conquered many evil lands. When Osiris died, he was buried right outside of his palace's bedroom window, but the next day his grave had disappeared and mysteriously changed into, what is referred to today as, an evergreen tree. Thus, began the tradition of going out on Horus/Osiris's birthday (December 25th) of each year, cutting down an evergreen tree, and bringing it inside the house to decorated it with various beautiful gold and silver ornaments, attempting to resurrect Osiris for the third time. As time passed, this tradition became more and more intense, because people felt a more desperate need, each passing year, to be under the governance of a king like the one and only good king, Osiris.

The Holy Bible, translated by King James, is an extraordinary piece of work, and it is probably the most widely read and most clearly written books in all North America; therefore, it seems almost sinister to attempt to change it. When something has been changed, is it really the same as it was initially? Is The Living Bible, The New American Standard, and The King James Bible really saying the same thing? Are people really trying to make the Holy Bible easier to read when they change it, or are people attempting to hide something that was overlooked, in the past, due to their lack of understanding of what was being said?

Jeremiah 10: 3-4, what does it mean, or better yet what does it say? Can anyone deny that this is the ritual people perform during the so-called "Christmas" season? Is this happening hundreds of years before "Jesus" is born? How can this be? Does Christmas really have something to do with "Jesus," or does "Jesus" have more to do with "Christmas?" Who is the heathen being referred to in Jeremiah 10: 2? Is it Israel? No, here, Israel is being warned not to be like the heathen; therefore, it is obvious that it is not the Israelite who is being referred to as the heathen.

Who is the heathen, then? Yes, it is Egypt! Nevertheless, when a person calls someone something evil, does that make that someone what that person called that someone? Abraham Lincoln, a famous attorney, long ago, asked a man, "if you called a dog's tail a leg, how many legs would a dog have?" "Five," the man answered. "No," replied the famous attorney, it has four." "You can call a tail anything you want to call a tail, but a dog only has four legs." Isn't that beautiful logic?

When Israel broke free from Egypt, many of the Egyptian customs were, by many, considered as vain. Although, many hundreds of years later, when the Romans and the Greeks entered and conquered (by whatever means they used) Egypt and the surrounding nations, many of the customs were considered quite logical. Therefore, they accepted them and implemented them in their new-found Christian faith.

Now, if a story was told to the reader today, and someone else came three thousand years later and told the reader an identical story, to whom would the reader attribute the origin of that story? When one studies world history and the different myths and legends throughout the world, including ancient Egyptian culture, one easily discovers that the first story ever told of a "Virgin Birth" was the story of an Egyptian queen, Isis. This story was told three thousand years before, even, the birth of the so-called Jesus (more than five thousand years ago it seems). Can the reader see the similarities between the names Jesus and Isis? In some religions, Jesus is referred to as Isa or Iesous. Can the reader see the similarities between Isis, Isa, and Iesous. Isis, this Egyptian virgin queen, was visited by her murdered husband, in the form of a spirit, when she conceived and gave birth to her holy son, who was born on December 25th and was called the "Son of the Sun-God."

To make a long story short (because the reader is expected to research this for him or herself), Horus/Osiris' grave, the first day after his burial, had mysteriously changed (over night) into a large evergreen tree. This is the birth which has caused so much controversy, and the very origin of what is referred to today as "Christmas." Three thousand years before the so-called Jesus (five thousand years ago), people would go out and find one of these special trees, bring it in their homes (Jeremiah 10), and decorate it as beautifully as they could, hoping the "Son of the Sun-God" would return and bring eternal peace to the world.

So, when some beautiful lost brothers and sisters approach you, attempting to deny the reader access to Christmas, insinuating that you have now accepted another religion other than Christianity, you should know what to say. Being of non-European descent (only if this applies to the reader), you should hit the ceiling at the insinuation that you cannot observe, enjoy, and love Christmas. Simply turn to that beautiful lost brother or sister and reply, "brother, or sister", the origin of Christmas is in Africa. Should all of that be ignored, because someone else, after this original story had been told for three thousand years, by non-European peoples, decided to create another story (obviously an exact replica) that denies non-Europeans any place in religious history and that claims proprietorship of Christmas, supported by a Holy Bible that contradicts this very claim in Jeremiah 10:3-4?"

TO CURSE A SON...

The King James Version has with good reason been termed 'the noblest monument of English prose.'" Its revisers, in 1881, expressed admiration for 'its simplicity, its dignity, its power, its happy turns of expression...the music of its cadences, and the felicities of its rhythm.' It entered, as no other book has, into the making of the personal character and the public institutions of the English-speaking peoples. We owe to it an incalculable debt (Cokesbury, 1951)."

Yet, the King James Version has grave defects. By the middle of the nineteenth century, the development of Biblical studies and the discovery of many manuscripts, more ancient than those upon which the King James Version was based, made it manifest that these defects are so many and so serious as to call for revision of the English translation" (Cokesbury, 1951, pp. iii, iv).

Thirty two Bible Scholars, securing the review and counsel of an "Advisory Board" of fifty representatives of the cooperating denominations, with a committee working in two sections, one dealing with the New Testament and one dealing with the Old Testament, they both determined that many conclusions in the Bible had to be changed. The changes, though, had to be scrutinized by each member of each section, and agreed upon by at least a two-thirds vote of the total membership of the committee, before becoming part of the new publication. The Revised Standard Version of the Bible, containing the New and Old Testaments, was authorized by vote of the National Council of the Churches of Christ in the U.S.A., in 1951.

The changes, not as one might think, were not changes in the language or dialect, but were changes in the misleading ideas that the Bible had previously suggested. To be exact, anywhere that Jesus was referred to as the only begotten Son of God, and anywhere in the four gospels that Jesus was depicted as rising up into a heaven whole body and soul were taken out, and were left out for nearly twenty-two full years. John 3:16, one of the foundations of the Christian belief, and Mark 16:9, Luke 24:51, were agreed upon to be removed. Ironically, many readers of the Holy Bible could not deal with this, and they insisted these excerpts be put back into the Bible, after over twenty years of them being left out.

However, this book is not meant to discredit any religion nor to discredit any religious text. Instead, this book seeks to accept, especially, the King James Version of the Holy Bible's Old Testament and to expound upon it, as much as necessary. It is to declare the New Testament somewhat of a fabrication and an almost direct copy (with the exception of the changing of names to protect the "guilty"), of the story of the virgin Isis, the good king Osiris, and the son of the Sun-God, Horus, to whom Christmas rituals were initially attributed, to whom belongs the credit for being the first carnal representation of the Father, the Son, and the Holy Spirit, and to whom the first holy birthday of December 25th was reserved.

Most adults (black, brown, red, yellow, and white) in the Christian churches of today actually believe in a black or red man with horns, a tail, and a pitchfork who lives underground and a white man with long white hair, a long white beard, and a staff who sits on a throne above the clouds. How foolish can an adult be? Nevertheless, this is their belief and their business, but these same adults, especially the pastors, ministers, and priests, are teaching their congregations, and pretending to believe themselves, that African Americans, Africans, and other dark-skinned peoples of the world are the result of a divine curse placed upon the descendants of Ham (one of the sons of Noah) for looking upon his father's nude body, while his father was drunk from wine. What is more horrible than adults, male and female, teaching themselves and their innocent little babies a ridiculous lie of this sort? Would you say nothing? How much confidence and self-esteem is being destroyed, in African-American children and other children of color, in all Christian churches and Christian oriented schools, because of this and similar teaching? An immeasurable amount, be assured!

The most important question, though, is "does the Holy Bible really say, that someone was cursed to have black skin, because of something Ham saw or did?" No, the Holy Bible, in no way says any such thing. Instead, the Bible, seems to insinuate that, because of the transgression of Noah's son, Noah's son's descendants were to be cursed with servitude or slavery, and this servitude was to be extended to the other two brothers (Japheth: the European; and Shem: the Semitic people or the Middle Easterner). They were to be the overseers.

Well, what exactly does the Bible say in Genesis 9:20-27? "And Noah began to be a husbandman, and he planted a vineyard: And he drank of the wine, and was drunken; and he was uncovered within his tent. And Ham, the father of Canaan saw the nakedness of his father, and told his two brethren without." First of all, any good reader must fully agree that, Noah's nakedness was uncovered, and the uncovering of Noah's nakedness is most definitely associated with Ham. This would be obvious to even a fifth-grade reader, but what does the Bible say about the uncovering of a person's nakedness? It has been said that if one continues to read any book, and continues to read, until that book has been read from cover to cover, it would be very difficult not to know what the whole book had said. Does the reader agree? If the answer is yes, then turn your King James Bible to the book of Leviticus and be liberated from a lie that has plagued people of color for hundreds of years. Leviticus 20:11 says, "And the man that lieth with his father's wife hath uncovered his father's nakedness." So, to uncover a person's nakedness means, according to the Holy Bible, to go to bed with that person's spouse. Leviticus 18:8 says, "The nakedness of thy father's wife shalt thou not uncover: it is thy father's nakedness." So, incest was the act or perpetration, but what was the curse or the result? Does incest produce blackness or black skin? Of course not! If so, according to some statistics and many rumors, one could easily assume that there should be at least one black child in almost one out of every twelve white families in America, Europe and South Africa. On the contrary, though, according to biology, incest can cause or help to produce a recessive gene, and a recessive gene can cause albinism, albino-ism, or simply albinos. An old belief is that "if a man marries a woman and they produce a female child; then, the wife dies and the man produces a male child with his daughter, by committing incest with his daughter; then, he dies, and the daughter produces children with her father's son, the children, from this point on, can be born totally void of color and with many other physical defects, because of the continued overuse of recessive genes (after the third generation of incest). There is an albino horse farm in Arizona. Here the creating of albino horses is quite common. There are three distinct cases of incest in the Holy Bible where white races were the results: (1) with Noah's wife and one of Noah's sons in Genesis 9:21; (2) with Jacob's wife and one of Jacob's sons in Genesis 49:4; (3) and with Lot and Lot's two daughters in Genesis 19:32-38. First of all, many reader's of the Holy Bible have never ask themselves why the father Noah, the original so-called Turk, has brown eyes and black hair; one son Ham, the original so-called African, has brown eyes and black hair; another son Shem, representing the so-called semite or Assyrian, has brown eyes and black hair; but the one and only son Japheth, the so-called European, different from his father and his other two brothers, has blue eyes and yellowish hair? If four people were marching, and three of them were so synchronized that their left feet all struck the ground simultaneously in unison, but at that same time, the fourth person's right foot would be striking the ground, who would be considered as being off-beat, the three in unison? No, of course not! If this was the case, Sgt. Carter would not be screaming at Gomer Pyle, he would be screaming at the rest of the men marching along with Gomer Pyle, would he not?

It is also obvious that after Lot died, both of his daughters, thinking there was no other person alive, mated with their own sons, and much more than three generations of incest were undergone. Ben-ami-mi was the result of this incident, and Benjamin was the result of the incident concerning Jacob. The origin of the word Benjamin means white and so does the origin of Ben-ami-mi.

It seems that just as European Americans have their demeaning and derogatory tales of Black people and there origin, saying that Blacks came from a divine curse or that Blacks came from monkeys and apes, because of their color, long arms and fingers, and thick lips; Blacks have tales that they tell their children and toss between each other as well. It appears that the Albinos, because of their recessive genes are believed, by many Blacks (Muslims and non-Muslims), to have been able to breed with the dog, and many believe they did mate with the dog, and this is supposedly why Europeans hair became straight; noses became long and narrow; bodies became elongated with short legs; why some of their women have seven and eight babies at one time; why they are excessively hairy; why they give off a dog-like smell when wet; and why they refer to the Creator as God, which is dog spelled backwards. Do not both of these stories sound utterly ridiculous? However, is it fair that one of these stories be heard by the entire world, but the other only be uttered in the African American ghetto alley-ways of North America, where only Blacks can hear them? Nevertheless, the Holy Bible does not say that Ham was cursed at all, but Genesis 9: 25 says, "Cursed be Canaan, a servant of servants shall he be unto his brethren." So what curse is being referred to here? The answer, of course, is forced servitude or slavery. However, the Bible never says that Ham was cursed black. So, it appears that the curse upon Ham's off-spring was slavery or servitude, while the result of prolonged acts of incest appears to be white skin, but it seems that because Whites could control the writing of history, they could, of course, reverse what they wanted to reverse and hide what they wanted hidden. This truth will anger many, but it is time for truth!

Due to continuous procrastination, on the part of the author, it has taken ten years to write this book; nevertheless, during this time, it has been contemplated how Dr. Frederick K. C. Price (a very brilliant pastor who appears to live in Los Angeles, California), might be mentioned in "Come To Life;" he is so well-loved and respected in the author's home. However, after his Sunday's television program (3 Jan 97) lecture, this dilemma was eradicated. The following is an actual letter to the Honorable Dr. Frederick K.C. Price or Los Angeles, California. However, the letter was probably never read on the air; although, it did meet the criteria specified by Dr. Price. It seems, though, that because of some of the things said by Dr. Price, after the letter was mailed, that he had read this letter. The letter in response to some of Dr. Price's television episodes is as follows:

Dearest Dr. Frederick K. C. Price:

You are well respected, admired, and loved in our home, as you are probably in most homes. Some of my wife's close relatives belong to your congregation. However, Dr. Frederick K. C. Price, on your Sunday television series (3 Jan 99), from information gathered from materials that either you selected or someone else selected for you, informed your congregation that Prophet Muhammad was White; Muhammad said women had an inferior mind, amounting to half that of men; and that Black Muslims have seemingly left one White man, Jesus (a devil according to Black Muslims, if he was White), for another White man, Muhammad (a devil, as well, according to Black Muslims, if he was White). This is beautiful logic, but it could be deceiving, especially when Dr. Price, you did not say that all other teachings, today, are similar; especially yours. Literature, today, tends to call things or people White who (or) that actually were Black, especially if they did something great. Could this possibly be what is referred to as "White Washed," Dr. Price? What color was Moses, when he placed his hand into his bosom and brought it out, it was "white," but when he placed it back in and brought it out, it had returned to its original color? Charlton Heston could not perform that miracle, in "The Ten Commandments," could he Dr. Price? Charlton Heston was already white, so this miracle was conveniently left out, knowing that most people do not read for themselves. Moses even lived among the Egyptians (Blacks) and was thought to be one of them.

In Genesis 21:21, did not Hagar (a black woman) go back to Egypt to find a wife for her son (Ishmael) from her own people? Abraham, being Semitic (half black and half white), and Hagar, being black, would probably produce a near black son. Do you not agree, Dr. Price? The descendants of Ishmael (7/8 Black) and his black wife were the original Arabs. Most nations have been lightened, due to European invasions, especially those in the Jordan Valley, by Romans, Greeks, Germans, British, you name it. What color are Farrakhan's armpits; his inner thigh? So, there were people of different shades, during Prophet Muhammad's time, this is what Islam is all about. Can you say the same thing about Jesus, who openly said he came to the Jews, and on one occasion referred to Greeks as dogs? Jesus told the Greek woman "it is not meet to take the children's bread, and cast it to the dogs." Did Jesus, ever in his life, according to what is written in your Bible, try to unite different races of people under one God (per se). Then why do Christians continue to talk of a trinity? Are we not all in the Father; and is not the Father in all of us? Did Jesus ever say (per se) that he was the father, the son, and the Holy Spirit? Jesus would never say that he was the father. Why would he never say this, Dr. Price?

Your Bible says specifically that the woman was made for the man, and that the man was not made for the woman (1 Corinthians 11:9). Does your Bible allow women to speak in church? In 1 Corinthians 14:34 "Let the women keep silence in the churches, for it is not permitted unto them to speak......and if they will learn (anything), let them ask their husbands at home." Has this been changed, Dr. Price? Can your women now speak in the churches? Did you give them that privilege, or did Christ, or Christ through Paul? The only problem with your sermon (3 Jan 99) is that, many might say that, it seems, you did not perform a fair comparison. You said with Christ or God (Gal. 3:28), there is neither Bond nor Free, male nor female, etc. All religions claim this of their Deity, God, or Savior. Why did you not use 1 Corinthians 14:34? That seems to be more of an equal comparison of male chauvinism or female dominance, does it not? What about women being made from only one of man's ribs? We've heard of Gabriel, Michael, Uriel, Raphel, etc., etc., but where are your female angels, Dr. Price (remember you are well love-and respected, now, these are merely questions)? What about your women, who are responsible for all the sin and the evil in the world, remember Eve? Solomon, (1 Kings 3:12) the wisest man in the Bible, according to your Bible, said "I find more bitter than death, the woman...the sinner shall be taken by her" (Ecclesiastes 7:26). The wisest man in the Holy Bible also said he had seen one good man in every one thousand men, but in the lot (all) of women he had found none (Ecclesiastes 7:28). This is your Bible, Dr. Price; the Hadith is not the Holy Qur'an. Jesus in the Holy Qur'an is referred to as the "Son of Mary," because of her holiness, but in your holy book, Jesus is called the "Son of God," and to many this implies fornication or adultery between God and Mary. Who is respecting the woman more, Dr. Price? Solomon says all women are bitter than death!

Muslims do not praise Prophet Muhammad because they feel he was not white or that they believe he may have been black. They praise him because of the Holy Qur'an, not the Hadith nor the Sunnahs. Muslims do not worship Prophet Muhammad, Dr. Price, as Christians worship Jesus; this is the whole misunderstanding and the total difference between Islam and Christianity (Ibn Abdullah Muhammad of Arabia was neither Allah nor the Son of Allah, rather the seal of all prophets, because his message, the Holy Qur'an, was memorized by his followers before Islam was preached in the streets, and it could not be destroyed, as was the teachings of Jesus who came before Muhammad with the same identical message, that was changed by the Romans). Muslims worship Allah through his "Holy Reading," the Holy Qur'an, revealed to Prophet Muhammad. Furthermore, Dr. Price, these may be white-washed writings that you are reading, is that not possible? Rationally thinking, who, indeed, would be bragging, or trying so desperately to convey to people that Muhammad was White, someone nearer to White or someone nearer to Black?

A racial thing has been going on as long as there have been different races, and the world did not begin with different races, according to Black Muslims, probably according to you, and according to Christians. Is this correct, Honorable Dr. Frederick K. C. Price?

In Your Holy Bible, does it not say that God created one blood and from that blood came all mankind? Does that mean that the first man and woman were white and that all other races came from them, Dr. Price? Can Whites produce black children, Dr. Price, and at what point were all or even half of the Arabs White? It seems they are as much of a mixture in Arabia and the surrounding areas, as African Americans are in the United States, and by means of the same circumstances.

What color was Gabriel, according to Hadith, according to Prophet Muhammad? Gabriel was jet black, according to Hadith and Prophet Muhammad. Black Muslims in America or any other African American did not write the Holy Bible or Holy Qur'an, and they have never changed a word in any of the translations of either. The Holy Qur'an, translated by A. Yusef Ali, does not read as the others (Maulana Muhammad Ali, A. Shakir, Muhammad Marmaduke Pickthall), written in other countries other than his home, where Prophet Muhammad was never accepted during his life (Just as the Romans never accepted Jesus, but now they are controlling the knowledge of Christ, how interesting). The other Holy Qur'ans, none written by African Americans, state plainly that man was made from black mud (Surah 15:28), in three different places in the same Surah, and it also says that the "Guilty Blue-eyed will be dealt with on judgment day (Surah 20:102). Blacks in America did not write that in those books nor did any black man write that; so, why do you suppose a person who was not Black write in the Holy Qur'an that man was made from black mud fashioned into shape? Read them for yourself, Dr. Price; and decide for yourself. You decide which is most likely to be true, (the one) or the other three or four which are identical.

Do you believe in a red man with tail, horns, and a pitchfork who lives underground (a single physical Devil, as your Christian Churches teach), Dr. Price? Do you realize that you have adults in your congregation who still believe in a red man who lives underground and that they were cursed Black, because someone looked at their father's naked rear when he was drunk? Is this not horrible?

You have been known to read different passages from different books to your congregation (e.g., The Legend of the Jews, a beautiful lecture where you revealed some horrible things that are being taught about people of color), and endeavors like these take more courage than Ministers of today have, this is well-agreed! However, there is a book just finished this year (1999) titled, "Come To Life," authored by DJWA, that has ended your crusade. You simply will not touch some of the issues in this book, Dr. Price, mainly the Hamitic Myth and the origin of the New Testament. However, you will receive the book, and you are dared to present it, just as you were dared to present this letter, which now appears in "Come To Life," in its entirety.

With Love and Respect,
Djwa

JUDAISM

LIFE

LIFE

Wisdom Of The Jewish PEOPLE

According to Dr. H. Spencer Lewis, in one of his books titled, "The Secret Doctrines of Jesus," the Bible simply does not contain the unadulterated words of Jesus the so-called Christ. According to Dr. Lewis, from 325 A.D. until 1870 A.D., twenty ecclesiastical or church council meetings were held, in which man alone decided upon the context (meaning) of the Bible. Self appointed judges in the four Lateran Councils expurgated (removed objectionable passages) and changed the sacred writings to please themselves. Thus, Jesus' personal doctrines, of the utmost, vital importance to every man, woman, and child, were buried in unexplained passages and parables, according to Dr. Lewis.

Jews are hated because they do not except Jesus as the Christ and are not ashamed to admit it? Do Jews have reasons to believe Jesus was not the Christ? It really seems as though they have many, according to history and according to many scriptures. Actually, because there are so many valid reasons, only a selected few really need to be mentioned, before the reader becomes totally bored with the reality of it all?

First of all, Deuteronomy 18:18-20, says that God would raise up a prophet (from their people) like Moses, and if that prophet would speak words, in God's name, which he was not ordained to speak, that prophet would die. Was Jesus like Moses? Did Moses recruit disciples to help him gather up the people and show them God's ways? Did Moses work miracles in secret and tell people not to mention this to anyone, for fear of what might happen? It seems, according to the Old Testament, that Moses went and met Pharaoh face-to-face, told him what he wanted him to do, and when Pharaoh refused, Moses gave his warning, and Egypt was plagued with the destruction that Pharaoh (or Caesar, Pontius Pilate, or Herod if they had been alive) could do nothing to stop. Why did Pharaoh not kill Moses, put him in a dungeon, or hang him on a cross? Right! He could not, because God sent Moses to do a job, and God's enemies have no power over God! If Jesus was God's Christ (Destroyer) why did he sneak around teaching secretly, away from the others who truly needed religious teaching: the European invaders?

The Bible plainly says that Jews continually reminded Jesus of the Law, so many Jews were still following the laws that Moses had brought them, and Jesus said that the ten commandments was basically the foundation of being righteous. So, what was Jesus' real mission? Was Jesus' mission merely to reconvert the Jews that had been caused to backslide, or were Jews expected to separate from this evil religion, or way of life, that had been imposed upon them by European invaders?

Read Maccabees 1:41-51, in the Catholic Bible, or in any Bible that has an Apocrypha, and discover that Israel was forced to eat swine, to discontinue circumcision, to forget the law, and to change all ordinances, not by Jesus (AS IT IS INSINUATED BY MANY), but by these European invaders who did not believe in nor thoroughly understand the lifestyle of the Jews. If then, after one has read Maccabees 1:41-51, and one agrees with who is responsible for the law being abolished, then the only question left concerning this particular matter is, "why do many people teach that Jesus came to change or get rid of the old law and/or to allow one to do some things, now, that God did not allow one to do in the past; especially if Jesus said, "I and the Father are one?"

Revelation 1:14-17, gives a description of Christ that many older African Americans, especially, have memorized. However, if Jesus had hair like pure wool, as white as snow, eyes as flames of fire, feet like fine brass, voice like that of a multitude, face like lightening, and a sharp two-edged sword coming out of his mouth, why would Judas have to kiss Jesus so that the murdering, thieving, raping, vulgar, invading soldiers, who had come into Israel with evil intentions, would know who Jesus was? Could Judas not have simply described Jesus to the murdering, thieving, raping, vulgar invaders?

Many people teach that Jews killed Jesus. Many people teach that Jesus came to save Jews from their sins, and they make no mention of the Europeans at all. This is total nonsense! Jews barely had any control over themselves at all, during this era. It appears that disbelieving invaders were now totally in charge of the livelihoods of all Jews in the Jordan Valley, and Jews almost had to request permission to breathe. Jesus was not the only Jew who was crucified. Many Jews were crucified before and after the crucifixion of Jesus.

Evidence points to the idea that many scores of years before Jesus was born, European soldiers were senselessly murdering Jewish males, viciously raping Jewish females, and stealing every valuable item the Jews possessed, and after Jesus was killed, this continued even more.

Nevertheless, if Jews were negligently breaking some of the laws, like working on the Sabbath or using the Lord's name in vain; how could God overlook all of this filth, horror, and viciousness perpetrated by one of his other races of people (against the entire nation of the Jews), and focus his attention toward someone who fixed a hole in his porch on the seventh day of the week, or shouted "GOD DAMN," when a filthy Roman soldier murdered his father and raped his mother? If there are any people who should have had a savior sent to them to save them from their sins, it seems, it should have been the Roman soldiers (who were obviously sinning)! The lighter side of this, though, is that the Europeans might be right! The way of God might just be that one travels throughout the world, wherever one wishes, and invades, deceives, destroys, kills, conquers, tortures, rapes, and enslaves, regardless of the pain and agony caused, until all who looks different are under their feet! Could this be the way of God?

Then, why should Jews accept European doctrines, after what Alexander, and the thirteen or more Antiochal kings who followed in Alexander's footsteps, did to Jews? Furthermore, how can Christians justify leaving Alexander out of the Bible, a very relevant figure, and then leaving all the other horrible debatable atrocities in the Bible, unless something was intended to be hidden? The Catholic Bible, with its fourteen books of the Apocrypha, seems more than proud to tell of Alexander, the so-called Son of Zeus, who is famous for striving to change the observance of the Mosaic laws, who had blue eyes, milky white skin, and flowing blonde hair, and who died when he was thirty-three years old. This famous man, with all these familiar attributes, sounds almost like Jesus himself, doesn't he? Is he really the Jesus Christians have been worshipping all these years?

In the book of Maccabees, in the Catholic Bible, in chapter seven, it shows the vicious mentality of the Greeks and their cruel oppression of the Jewish people, over two-hundred years before their European brothers, the Romans, took over. In Maccabees 7:1-13, it says that a mother and her seven sons were being tortured because they refuse to eat pork, which is divinely forbidden in their Mosaic laws. Each of them, one at a time, were told to eat the pork; when they refused, one at a time, they were scalped, they all had their hands and feet chopped off, all had their tongues cut out, and all were thrown into a giant skillet and fried like fish until smoke filled the air from their burning bodies. The Greeks had giant skillets constructed to fry the Jews, when they would not forsake the laws of their forefathers, but many naive nonreaders tell you, today, that Jesus changed the laws of the Old Testament and started a New Testament. What a horrible lie! That is not what Jesus said in Matthew 5; 17-22.

Still, what kind of human being could fry another human being in a giant skillet, and stand around and, not only look on, but enjoy the smell as well. Maybe the question should be, should these perpetrators be called human beings at all? Nevertheless, many people teach that the Son of God (maybe they mean the Son of Zeus: Alexander) changed some of the laws of his father, and now allowed all people to place all their sins on this Son's back. Allowing all of their horrible sins to be place on the back of one innocent human being is almost as vicious and horrendous as frying someone in a giant skillet (obviously two ideas from the same origins). So now, it is obvious where this belief came from. Yes, and of course, the Protestant, just like other Christian Bibles, was translated from the Greek Bible; although, they ironically left out four hundred years of history, which included, who else other than the great European hero, "Alexander the Great?" So, when the question as to why Jews do not accept Jesus as God's Christ or the Son of God, ask them to please give the Jews a break? Why should they?

The Sacred Scriptures say that Yeshua (Jesus) was impaled. The Holy Bible says, in some places, that Jesus was hung on a cross, but in Acts 5:30 it says Jesus was hanged on a tree. Some Holy Assemblies teach that Jesus never was hung to death at all, and some religions teach that Jesus (Isa) was stabbed in the heart and formed a cross with his own body, and no one could move his body from the wall where it was pinned for nearly three days, until his true father Joseph (who up to this point had never claimed Jesus, because of his marriage to another woman, other than Mary, who had never told that Joseph was Jesus' father, to avoid both their deaths) came to claim the body. As the little country boy said, "Will somebody please make up muh galdurn mind?"

A book which cost only five dollars can be purchased from the Abelard Reuchlin Foundation, in Kent, Washington, (P.O. BOX 5652, KENT, WA 98031) which offers a reward of $1,416.19 to anyone who can prove that the authors named in this chapter did not write the books of the New Testament.

The insinuation apparently is that the New Testament was written from what was already known and/or written, after these people who wrote it read also the already existing Old Testament. It appears that they read it, and attempted to piece together a believable fulfillment, but ultimately in writing a fulfillment, very gracefully achieved creating the deception of appearing to be centering it around a man who tried to stand up to them and they murdered, but writing it secretly about men whom they praised: Alexander the Great and the Antiochal Kings that followed him.

Are these little books, written by Dr. H. Spencer Lewis and The Abelard Reuchlin Foundation lying or telling the whole truth? Does the reader need fifteen hundred dollars? Has the reader read Joshua 10:13 and 2 Samuel 1:18? Where is the Book of Jasher? It certainly is not in the Old Testament or the New Testament! Nevertheless, if one goes to the library of one's home town, though, one will find the Book of Jasher. One might also discover that Jasher was the scribe who traveled with Moses; who was writing down everything that took place during the interaction between Moses, Aaron, and Pharaoh. Learn also the reasons the Book of Jasher gives why Pharaoh was really chasing the Israelites, just prior to the Red Sea opening up for the Israelites to cross over to safety. According to the Book of Jasher, Pharaoh was trying to catch up with the children of Israel to get his money back that they had stolen from him. One should read the Book of Jasher.

The Abelard Reuchlin Foundation, apparently, has done its home work. The Author himself wanted to earn that quick little fifteen hundred dollars ($1416.19), but discovered that it was not as easy as he expected. However, after studying intensely, the author realized how well it followed, but then marveled over how such a monstrous lie could be hidden, not only so well, but so long.

According to the Abelard Reuchlin Foundation, P.O. Box 5652, Kent WA 98031, they will give anyone a $1416.19 reward if that person or those persons can prove that the true authors of the New Testament are NOT listed on the following page.

TRUE AUTHORSHIP OF THE NEW TESTAMENT

NAME OF BOOK	DATE WRITTEN	TRUE AUTHORS
The Original Mark	60 C.E.	Lucius Calpurnius Piso
Matthew	70-75 A. D.	Arius Calpurnius Piso
The Present Mark	75-80 A. D.	Arius Calpurnius Piso
Luke	85-90 A. D.	A. C. Piso & Pliny
John	105 A. D.	Justus Calpurnius Piso
Acts Of The Apostles	96-100 A. D.	Chap. 1-15, A. C. Piso & Justus Chap. 16-17, By Justus; Chap. 18-28, Some Justus, Some Pliny
Romans	100 A. D.	Proculus Calpurnius Piso
I Corinthians Galatians & Ephesians	100-103 A. D.	Pliny
I Corinthians, Philippians & Colossians	106-107 A. D.	Justus & His Son Julianus'
I Timothy	105 A. D.	Pliny
II Timothy	107 A. D.	Justus
I & II Thessalonians	105-110 A. D.	Justus With The Help Of Julianus And His Nephew Silanus
Titus	103-105 A. D.	Pliny
Philemon	105-110 A. D.	Justus With The Help Of Julianus
James	110 A. D.	Justus
I and II Peter	110-115 A. D.	Proculus
I, II, & III John	110-115 A. D.	Julius Calpurnius Piso
Jude	110-115 A. D.	Julius
Revelations	136-137 A. D.	Julius
Hebrews	140 A. D.	Flavius Arrianus (Arrian) AKA Appian, Younger Grandson Of Piso

Nevertheless, with all this damaging knowledge, and all this knowledge that contradicts popular teaching with such unbelievably polite dignity, the Jewish people leave the Christians in peace with their ignorance. This knowledge could very well completely tear down the foundation of the Christian belief. However, the Jewish people are being very humble and use this knowledge only to steer their own people in the right direction. Maybe it is wrong to insinuate this, but it seems that if others had this much destructive knowledge against Judaism, they would use it to destroy the Jews. However, the Jews seem comfortable just knowing the truth, instead of persecuting others with that truth. The author must admit that the Jews set a good example of a people who want peace.

This is the difference between interpretation of sacred or holy scriptures and historical research and the imparting of information. One cannot deny that this is, indeed, a revelation, and only the closed-minded will turn his or her head and ignore this, especially if he or she cannot prove otherwise, but can, in fact, confirm this assertion, with the minimal amount of research.

However, Jews, as well as others, have been criticized for their interpretation of the Holy Scriptures. Although the interpretations flow convincingly, one can still detect racism and male chauvinism. If one wishes to read some of the beliefs of some Jews, one might read "The Legend of the Jews." It is believed that Adam was married twice: once to a woman "Lilith," who flew away from him, it appears, because they were created equal, and that would not work and once to "Eve," who, it appears, is responsible for all the evil and death in the world, but because she was taken from man, she is somewhat less than he is.

A really funny and wise interpretation of the incident concerning Noah and Satan and the making of the first wine, though, should be read by all. "Let us go into partnership in this business of planting a vineyard," asked Satan? Noah agreed with Satan that this was a good idea! Satan, thereupon, slaughtered a lamb, and then, in succession, a lion, a pig, and a monkey. The blood of each as it was killed; he made to flow under the vine. Thus, Satan conveyed to Noah what the qualities of the wine are: (1) before man drinks of it, he is as innocent as a lamb; (2) if he drinks of it modestly, he feels as strong as a lion; (3) if he drinks more of it than he can bear, he resembles the pig; and (4) if he drinks to the point of intoxication, he behaves like the monkey, he dances around, sings, talks obscenely, and knows not what he is doing (Vol. 1, p. 168). Is this not beautiful logic? It is a somewhat child-like interpretation, but very clever.

African Americans and other people of color take offense to others' interpretations concerning how people of color came to be. This can be understood though, if one considered the problems Jews had encountered with the Egyptians (the descendants of Ham). Who would not seek to harm and/or get away from a people who had enslaved them for 400 years. To believe that Hamites were superior would be to believe that Jews were inferior; therefore, it seems, Jews, although being Semitic (at one time half black and half white), chose to worship, in part, their white ancestry, without worshipping or even acknowledging their white ancestors. Although, now, it is obvious that the Jews, especially of Western world, are closer to the "White End" of the "Color Spectrum" than the "Black End," and thus they think. This can be detected, upon reading excerpts from "The Legend of the Jews," concerning Ham. Although, Jews do admit that Canaan, not Ham, was cursed, still have their own conclusions about what that curse was. "The descendants of Ham through Canaan, therefore, have red eyes, because Ham looked upon the nakedness of their father; they have misshapen lips, because Ham spoke with his lips to his brothers about the unseemly condition of his father; they have twisted curly hair, because Ham turned and twisted his head around to see the nakedness of his father; and they go around naked, because Ham did not cover the nakedness of their father" (p. 169). This, however, is just a mild version of the Ham interpretation, the Jews have reasons why black males have long sex organs and the whole bit. They really get into it; although, some people of color dislike this harsh interpretation and really take offense to it! This is merely interpretation, and has very little to do with fact, the Holy Bible does not say this, as a matter of fact, it supports just the opposite.

ISAIAH'S WORD

WHO REALLY, AND WHERE, IS IMMANUEL?

When members of races of color attempt to point out that Jesus might have been a man of color, they encounter many ignorant, hateful, and oftentimes totally ironic responses, even from their own people.

Usually forgetting that people are talking about Jesus the man, and not God the spirit, some ignorant or naive Caucasian or African American Christians will say "God does not have a color." Now, this is about as ignorant and as ironic as one can get. Everyone else who lived in the region where Jesus lived had a color. If a person or thing exists or has ever existed, a color can be attributed to it. First of all, no one mentioned God; the subject is Jesus: a man who walked among other men and women and could be seen by the human eye.

The Bible says in Matthew 19:16 "Good Master, what good thing shall I do, that I may have eternal life?" Jesus, then, responded, according to the Bible, from his own mouth, "Why callest thou me good? There is none good (but one), that is, God." This is plain enough for a simpleton to understand, but there is much more to confirm that God is the father, God being depicted as more powerful than Jesus. Matthew 24:36 says, "But of that day and hour knoweth no man, no, not the angels of heaven, but my father only." Ironically, though, Christians attempt to confuse the issue, forgetting that they are the ones who said Jesus was a Jew, and if he did not have a color, he's the only Jew that does not have a color.

Please remember that the Jews that Hitler persecuted, the so-called Jew who lived among, mixed with, and intermarried with Europeans for many hundreds of years, after being chased out of the region of Jerusalem, looks much more European than the people who lived in Jerusalem during Jesus' time. Matthew 26:48 says, "Now he who was betraying him gave them a sign, saying 'Whomever I shall kiss, He is the one; seize him." Now if Jesus did not have a color, why did Judas have to kiss him so that the Roman soldiers would know who Jesus was? Why did Judas simply not say, "It is the man who has no color, he is just an illustration?" He looks like a picture in a coloring book which has not been colored. This is foolish, huh? Yes it is! Just as it is obvious that Jesus looked just like all the rest of the Jews of his time, and if he had been a Roman traitor or had any Roman blood in his veins at all, or was Chinese, or Indian, or Greek, surely someone would have remembered to mention this very relevant detail, with support, also, of a trifle bit of corroborating lineage, perhaps.

Christians, especially European Americans, say it does not matter what color Jesus was. If this is true, why is he depicted as a European and not a black haired, brown-eyed, olive-skinned man from the Middle East? Why do they want to teach in American public schools, to little Black, Brown, Red, and Yellow children; that the creator of the entire universe has only one son, and he was White? If it truly does not make a difference what color Jesus actually was, why won't European Americans paint Jesus' pictures to look, as much as is humanly possible, the way Jesus actually looked? This is if it really doesn't matter to European Americans. The truth, it seems, is that European Americans are the only ones who really have a motive to control the way people, especially children of America, conceive Jesus. Why won't European Americans teach that Jesus was a Middle Easterner and looked like all the rest of the Middle Easterners of his time? Why won't they teach that Jesus had brown eyes, black hair, and dark skin? Does not the truth make it right, and does not that which is not true keep it from being right?

Christians say Jesus wanted to die on the cross. They say he wanted to die for the sins of others. Then, why was he constantly hiding? Why was he begging God to keep this from happening to him? In Matthew 26:36-44, Jesus is asking God if it is possible to escape this fate. Jesus asked this three times. Jesus is a man who had never done a single thing wrong in his entire life, according to Christians. According to scripture, Jesus had only done right for everyone he met? Where is God's compassion and sympathy? Is this not God's son? Jesus hides throughout his entire life from the wrath of Europeans and European justice. This holy man is begging, not just once, but three times, concerning one incident. Why do Christians teach their children to do right, to say excuse me, thank you, you're welcome, forgive me, and all other forms of courtesies and politeness, if this does not mean a thing in the eyes of God? This is such a contradiction in teachings! Moreover, why, when Jesus was hanging on the cross, did Jesus accuse God of abandoning him, if this was all in the bargain or the plan (according to the Bible)?

Did God say the word "Jesus" means that Jesus should die for his people, or did he say Jesus shall save his people from their sins? Who really decided Jesus should die for all, so that everyone else should live, and why? Who really decided on this particular lie to tell the people, after Lazarus had been brought back to life, according to the Bible? According to John 11:48-54, after Lazarus had been brought back to life by Jesus, according to the Bible, the chief priests and the Pharisees became afraid, thinking that if too many people followed Jesus, the Romans might decide to kill everyone and take the whole nation away from them. Therefore, Caiaphas, the chief priest, devised the plan soon after Lazarus had been revived to life, to make Jesus a martyr and a hero to the people who followed him, by killing him and declaring that Jesus, not only, died for his people but for all people. Then from that day forward, they took counsel to put Jesus to death. Jesus, apparently, not ready to die, walked no more openly among the Jews, according to the Bible (John 11:48-54). Christians, though, teach that God meant for Jesus to die. Do they know the truth, or are they just being ironic, trying to see just how much nonsense people will really believe, before they decide to read the Bible for themselves.

Some people say that Jesus in the New Testament is the Immanuel that Isaiah prophesied about in Isaiah 7:14-22. Does one see how conveniently some people resort to the Old Testament, when they think it will support their beliefs? However, when a person shows them Leviticus eleven and Deuteronomy fourteen, where the Bible says that eating the flesh of hogs or even touching a dead hog is forbidden, they say, "that's in the Old Testament." See how conveniently Christians use or reject the Old Testament. If it condemns Christianity, Christians complain, "that's in the Old Testament," but if it helps them, they brag that it is in the Old Testament. How sinister can a person allow him or herself to be?

Nevertheless, was Jesus really Immanuel? The fact is that Jesus was never once called Immanuel, nor did he answer to this name, during his lifetime or, even, anywhere in the Bible! The word Immanuel is in the Bible only a few times, and it is not even spelled the same way, in some of those places! If someone told you that a person was predicted to come that was named George, which meant he would be a famous artist. However, the person who showed up was a man named Kelvin, whose name meant he was to be a famous acrobat; would that be the fulfillment of the prediction? Can anyone be this foolish? It just does not follow, does it?

Well, what about Matthew 1:21-23, which says, "And she shall bring forth a son, and thou shalt call his name JESUS: for he shall save his people from their sins. Now all this was done, that it might be fulfilled which was spoken of the Lord by the prophet, saying, Behold a virgin shall be with child, and shall bring forth a son, and they shall call his name Emmanuel, which being interpreted is, God with us. This is totally non-sequitur, which means, it simply does not follow. Emmanuel, here, is even spelled with an "E," instead of an "I;" as Immanuel is in the Old Testament. The meanings though of Jesus and Immanuel, regardless of how either is spelled, have totally different meanings! One means to save people from their sins, and the other means God with us!

Moreover, according to Isaiah 7:14-15 it says: "Therefore the Lord himself shall give you a sign; Behold a virgin shall conceive, and bear a son, and shall call his name Immanuel. Butter and honey shall he eat, that he may know to refuse the evil, and choose the good. Verses eighteen and nineteen tells of the presence of Bees throughout the whole land. Furthermore, according to Isaiah 7:21-22, the Bible states, "And it shall come to pass in that day, that a man shall nourish a young cow, and two sheep; And it shall come to pass, for the abundance of milk that they shall give he shall eat butter: for butter and honey shall everyone eat that is left in the land." This is very detailed prophecy, is it not? No place in the New Testament, during the life and times of Jesus, is it mentioned that Jesus ate butter and honey until he knew to refuse the evil and choose the good. According to many people, Jesus always knew everything from birth; at least, this is the implication. Furthermore, there is no place in the New Testament where all the people who were left in the land were eating butter and honey, because of the abundance of milk and honey. This is a very important detail to leave out, is it not? As a matter of fact, according to the New Testament, Jesus fed five thousand men and many women and children with two little fish and five loaves of bread (Matthew 14:17), and on other occasions Jesus fed many followers. Milk and honey were to be abundant during Immanuel's time! Where was all this milk and honey; if Jesus was indeed Immanuel?

Muhammad's

True Message ?

Islam means total submission to Allah and all that is right. Of course, Prophet Muhammad had the right idea: all men are brothers; women should be equals, not property of their husbands, and should be able to choose their own husbands; one God (Allah); a divine diet; constant prayers; and strict observance and enforcement of God's law.

However, Muhammad and his followers were persecuted as badly as Jesus and his followers. Moreover, Muhammad's followers, like Jesus', after Muhammad's death, suffered continued persecution. One should ask oneself, would one throw a man out of one's house and then hang his or her picture up in one's living room, and start teaching his or her belief in one's own household, after throwing them out? Of course not!

The religion that Muhammad was trying to introduce was going to hurt a lot of people's pocketbooks, livelihoods, leisure time, and old habits in general. Muslims say that Muhammad was the last and final prophet, because the messages of the prophets before him had been tampered with, and some had been altered altogether, namely the message of Jesus the Messiah, by the Romans. However, if it is true that Muhammad's message has not been tampered with, then why are most women in Arabia not allowed to drive; are not educated the same as males; why are some Arabs filthy rich and some are dirt poor; why is the annual pilgrimage to Mecca being totally commercialized; why isn't the scripture of the Holy Qur'an being adhered to and abided by; and last but not least, how did the story of the virgin Mary with a son named Jesus get into the Holy Qur'an? This is a story almost identical to the story of Isis who was pregnant with Horus, running from the stalking Typhon?

Arabs owned slaves scores of years after Muhammad's death, but called themselves Muslim. Where was the respect for Bilal? Arabs conspired with Europeans during the Slave-trade, and they called themselves Muslim.

There are at least four different translations of the Holy Qur'an: A. Shakir, Yusef Ali, Marmaduke Pickthall, and Muhammad Ali, but Ironically, Muslims still insist that the Holy Qur'an has not been tampered with. This is a lie! It has been tampered with, to the extent of an almost total corroboration between the ones who compiled the Holy Qur'an and the ones who compiled the Bible: Shem and Japheth if you will. In the Holy Bible, Remember in Genesis 9: 27 it says, "God shall enlarge Japheth, and he shall dwell in the tents of Shem; and Canaan, the son of Ham, shall be his servant." Have controlling greedy Muslims been corroborating with controlling greedy Christians, for the sake of wealth all along?

The Holy Qur'an has been translated by M. H. Shakir, Malauna Muhammad Ali, Muhammad Marmaduke Pickthall, and of course, A. Yusef Ali. Three of these translations read identical, but one (A. Yusef Ali's) reads differently. Of Course, now, King Fahd, one of the most capitalistic men on earth, is personally endorsing A. Yusef Ali's version. Remember, Muhammad was never accepted in his own country. Why is King Fahd not publishing any of the other versions? Perhaps it's because of Surahs like Surah 5:51; Surah 15: 26, 28, 33; and Surah 20:101-102.

Just to be perfectly clear, no African American is responsible for translating any Holy Qur'an. Nevertheless, three of the translations in Surah 5:51 state: "Oh ye who believe! Do not take the Jews and the Christians for friends; they are friends of each other; and whoever amongst you who take them for friends; then surely he is one of them; surely Allah does not guide the unjust people. This Surah is basically the same in all translations, with the exception of a few words, but the Irony of it all is that the one that reads differently, in every case, is the one translated by Yusef Ali, similar to one of four persons singing out of tune or marching out of rhythm.

In Surah 15: 26 it states, "And certainly; we created man of clay that gives forth sound, of black mud fashioned into shape." Verse twenty eight says, "And when your Lord said to the angels: Surely I am going to create a mortal of the essence of black mud fashioned into shape. Verse thirty three Iblis (Satan) said, I am not much that I should make obeisance to a mortal who Thou hast created of the essence of black mud fashioned in shape." What would it benefit a person, who was not black, to say that man was created from black mud three times, if it was a lie? Nevertheless, A Yusef Ali's version does not say black anywhere in those verses. Is this not strange?

Finally, in each translation except A. Yusef Ali's, in Surah 20:101-102 it says, "Abiding in this (state), and evil be it for them to bear on the day of resurrection. On the day when the trumpet shall be blown; and we will gather the guilty, blue-eyed, on that day." Why do you think the Arabs took this out? Could it be because they have mixed with Europeans, to the extent that some of them now have eyes as blue as any European? This might not be true, but it is a very good assumption. Another good assumption is that America and Europe would not have anything to do with Arabia, if they left things like this in the Holy Qur'an, especially since so many people of all colors are accepting Islam as the religion of God. Nonetheless, the Holy Qur'an has been tampered with. Furthermore, some of the same things that Christians and Greeks stole from Africa and put in their Holy Books as having come from their prophets, one finds in the Holy Qur'an being attributed to Prophet Muhammad. Is this a coincidence or not? The story of the virgin Maryam, in the Holy Qur'an, is more like the story of Isis, from Egypt, than the Christian's story of the virgin. The Muslims story of Mary; down to the virgin hiding out in the wilderness and giving birth to the holy son is identical to that of Isis'. Remember, Muslims were the last conquerors of Egypt? This brings about the question, "to what extent will Shem and Japheth go, to keep Ham as their servant, but to use any portion of Ham's history which aids in delivering their religious message? Are things becoming more comprehendible now?

Finally, why won't Muslims admit how Prophet Muhammad (May the Peace and the Blessings of Allah be Upon Him) died? Many say he became sick of heart, when he realized he could not teach all of the evil ones Islam. What about the ones who were killed, under the orders of Muhammad, because they refused to accept Islam? Many say he died a natural death. How could that be? It is recorded that Muhammad was so sick the last several months of his life; he barely could tolerate standing. Islam allows a husband to marry up to four wives, if the husband can afford them, and then there are many stipulations (rules) concerning having up to four wives (e.g., if a husband spends four hours a day with one, he has to spend four hours per day with the others, if he buys one a handkerchief, he has to buy one for them all, etc.). It is believed that Prophet Muhammad never accepted another wife, as long as Cadijah, his wife of over twenty years, was alive, but was not quite the same after her death. However, he had as many as eleven wives and also fell in love with a Jewish woman, after the death of Cadijah; although, the Holy Qur'an allows only four. Many Muslims will argue, saying, "He was the prophet, and he was allowed more wives than other ordinary believers." Is this permissible act written anywhere?

How can anyone, especially a wise prophet, trust any female who has had most of the male members of her family killed: her father, brothers, cousins, older sons, uncles, older nephews, and grandfathers; regardless of what anyone is trying to do for her, or what anyone is trying to give her? Rumors are, Muhammad was poisoned and lived in pain and agony the last few years of his life. Why do Muslims appear ashamed to admit this? This still does not take away from the amazing results his beautiful message has had upon the world and upon the lives of many beautiful human beings. Furthermore, some Arab Muslims won't admit why their racial colors vary, and why some of them have Greek features.

Around 1986, on a well known university campus, an African American male and an Arabian male, in the midst of about eight to ten people listening, were arguing about the many evil accomplishments of "Alexander the Great." The African American was telling the Arabian that many Arabs got their Greek features from the fact that Alexander and his mighty army conquered many parts of the Arabian Peninsula. The African American proceeded to say that Alexander took 10,000 men and, for one year, tried to rebuild many parts of Babylon, very near to Bagdad. The Arab brother became very defensive and responded, "brother, brother, sure, many soldiers, many soldiers they came, but we did not have weapons, and they went back." This is word for word (verbatim) what the Arab brother said. The African American male laughed loudly and said, "right, thousands of blood-thirsty, horny men road horses, some walked in dust, sand, and through horse manure for seven hundred miles, and when they arrived in your country and saw all those thousands of beautiful women and girls and helpless weaponless men; they went back. Sure, urinate on my head, and tell me it's raining." This is what he said word-for word. "They went inside of you my brother!" One cannot imagine the laughter!

Nevertheless, many converted orthodox Muslims will admit that they were especially liberated in many ways by the Islamic stories of the birth of Mary and the story of Jesus in the Garden of Gethsemane: (1) A pregnant woman, upon visiting a holy prophet, was promised a holy child. When the child was born, the child was a female child, and the mother believing that a female child could not be a holy child, put the child up for adoption. Of all the people who did not have children, who were allowed to shoot arrows to see who would adopt the child, Zachariah, the eventual father of Ya-Ya (John the Baptist), shot his arrow further than anyone, and became the one who would adopt and raise the girl baby, that he would later name Mary. The Amazing thing is that Zachariah found out later that Mary was, indeed, a holy child. He said that sometimes he would take food to Mary's chambers, and she would already be eating Quail and Manna, the same food the Israelites were fed in the wilderness with Moses. When Mary was asked where the food came from, she answered that Allah was feeding her. It appears that Allah fed Mary until she became clean enough to conceive the Messiah, and once Mary was told that she would have a child without a man touching her, she conceived Jesus through faith alone, and this is why Muslims call Jesus the son of Mary. They are recognizing that Mary was holy. Isn't this beautiful?

The second story supports the scripture in the Holy Qur'an which states that "they think they crucified him, but of a certainty, they did not." When Jesus was praying in the Garden of Gethsemane, and Peter had been left to watch for the stalking Roman soldiers, Islam teaches that Jesus prayed to God (Allah) three times, making the same identical request each time. Jesus, a man who had never done anything wrong, a man who had gone out of his way and put his life on the line to help others, a man who had never even known a woman (according to the Christian's Holy Bible), a man who was born holy, a man who had never sinned asked the father of all mankind, "if there is any way for this cup to pass me by, then let it pass me by, but if there is no way for this cup to pass me by then let thy will be done." It has been said that with God, all things are possible. After Jesus went back twice and found Peter sleep and confronted him, the third prayer, apparently reveal a way that the cup could pass Jesus by. After Jesus prayed the third time, "if there is any way for this cup to pass me by, then let it pass me by, but if there is no way for this cup to pass me by then let thy will be done," when Jesus rose from prayer, there was a man standing next to him who had been sent to Jesus, by God, from the nearest prison. It is said that this man was guilty of committing many vicious crimes against God and man. When Jesus turned and looked at the man, the man's facial features began immediately to resemble the features of Jesus' face, and the more Jesus looked upon this man, the more the attributes of Jesus' was cast upon and unto the man. The man was so hypnotized by Jesus that he could only follow the command of Jesus to return to the disciples acting as a hypnotized zombie, and displaying the minimal amount of power. This is why Muslims believe Jesus was moving so slowly and saying so little when the Roman soldiers came down upon them, when in reality Jesus was very talkative. This man was he who was crucified, and this is why it was believed that Jesus was really crucified, because it was made to look as though it had actually happened, when Jesus actually departed in the Garden of Gethsemane in good health and in one piece.

The reader might also be interested enough to read the story of the people who were exiled in the caves so long that they were almost unbearable to look upon, the story of the birth of Jesus, the story of Moses and the Cow, the Elephant, and the story of Zhul Kharnain, the story of the building of a great wall to protect people from Gog and Magog.

This story of Jesus in the Garden of Gethsemane might sound as if Muslims made this little story up to support their belief in Jesus, but there is another story similar to this. This story is told by Barnabas, a former companion of St. Paul, in the Gospel of Barnabas, hidden for many years in the library of the Pope in Rome, Italy, until it was finally discovered in the fourth century. According to the Gospel of Barnabas (verses 214-217, pp. 262-264); "Jesus was praying in the garden, according to his custom of bowing his knees a hundred times and prostrating himself on his face. When the soldiers with Judas drew near to the place where Jesus was, Jesus heard the approach of many people, wherefore in fear, he withdrew into the house. The eleven disciples were then sleeping. Then God, seeing the danger of his precious servant, commanded Gabriel, Michael, Rafael, and Uriel, his ministers, to take Jesus out of this world." Jesus, according to the Gospel of Barnabas, was taken out of a south window by the angels and placed in the third heaven where he would bless God for evermore. Does this not sound more like the God that you are worshipping, one who will not allow your body any harm as long as you are trying to be righteous?

Judas, then, entered the house and entered the chamber where Jesus had been taken from. The eleven disciples were still sleeping. "Whereupon, the wonderful God acted wonderfully insomuch that Judas was so changed in speech and in face to be like Jesus that we believed him to be Jesus. And he, having awakened us, was seeking where the Master was. Whereupon we marveled, and answered: 'Thou, Lord, art our master; hast thou now forgotten us?' And Judas, smiling, said: 'Now are ye foolish; that know not me to be Judas Iscariot!' And as he was saying this, the Roman soldiers came in and seized him, because he looked in every way like Jesus." The other disciples were so shocked by all of this, they fled, some naked. Judas was beaten ferociously, spat upon, kicked, mocked, and bound. "Judas answered: (p. 266) 'Sir, believe, me, if thou put me to death, thou shalt do a great wrong, for thou shalt slay an innocent person; seeing that I am Judas Iscariot, and not Jesus, who is a magician, and by his art hath so transformed me.'" "But God (p. 267), who had decreed the issue, reserved Judas for the cross, in order that he might suffer that horrible death to which he had sold another." Is this not wild?

Many Orthodox Muslims say Jesus is not dead, but Jesus said out of his own mouth in the Holy Qur'an that he had been caused to die (Surah 5:117), in all translations, except A. Yusef Ali.

Nevertheless, Muslims, after Prophet Muhammad taught them all that he taught them, allowed themselves to be divided. Now there are Shiite and Sunnai, and they are killing each other. Muslims claim that Arabs and Persians are responsible for the division, could they really be so ashamed not toadmit that the Europeans did it over 400 years ago, just as the Europeans divided many cultures and many religions!

After 1492, when Columbus sailed the ocean blue, Europeans spread the influence of their religion and culture to other countries like "wildfire," causing extraordinary division in every country they entered. Thus, the questions become, "what truths concerning the Holy Prophet Muhammad are being suppressed, and what lies to support falsehoods are being enforced, even within the Islamic teachings, because of this influence? Is it coincidental that Christianity, Islam, and Hinduism all have a trinity: Christianity of course has God the Father, God the Son, and God the Holy Spirit; Hinduism has Brahman the "Creator," Krishna or Vishnu the "Sustainer" and Shiva the "Destroyer;" and Islam has Allah, Muhammad, and Gabriel. Hummmmmm! How interesting?

THE OLD EGYPTIAN

IS IT SO FOOLISH TO WORSHIP LIFE?

What evil picture of God have Christians, Muslims, Jews, Catholics, etc., seemingly, painted in their minds, so as to appear not to trust God? "God is not a man, that he should lie; neither is he the Son of Man, that he should repent: hath he said, and shall he not do it? Or hath he spoken, and shall he not make it good" (Holy Bible, Numbers, 23:19) Does it make sense for God, the creator of the heavens, the earth, and all within, to give each unsuspecting innocent individual the precious gift of life, make ordinances, laws, rules, etc. known to those individuals, and no matter whether one follows God's law or not, God will viciously and unfairly take that life back whenever God decides, regardless of what. This makes sense, if one was referring to the Devil. When referring to God, it makes more sense that God would give one the precious gift of life; then, when one proves one does not want that precious gift of life, God would then, and only then, and usually because the subject is experiencing unbearable pain, be forced to accept that life back! By not abiding by God's laws, regardless of the reason; and by breaking as many of God's commandments as possible; people are forced, by means of discomfort and pain due to these transgressions, to pray for death; and when this is done, and, by means of this, one is actually begging God to take this life back.

Many Christians, Jews, Catholics, and Muslims have learned, or better yet, been taught to subconsciously not trust God, and it seems subliminally, by means of this vicious lie that God betrayed his only son, and allowed his enemies to torture him. Therefore, it seems, many subconsciously mistrust God, believing that no matter how one lives, there is still a chance that one might be crushed by a Mack Truck at anytime for nothing! This is horrible! How can one be satisfied with his or her religion, living in such fear? What has God done to make people think that God won't protect them from evil, as long as they practice righteousness? People closely related to another person, by kinship or friendship, might not know what that person is guilty of, when that person meets an untimely, and oftentimes horrible death, but it is nonetheless recorded in time, space, and many times in the minds of those who see and do not tell! People like to hear this, so they can say, "well what about children?" Many children die who haven't done anything to anyone! There is a beautiful story in the Muslim's Holy Qur'an about Moses traveling with the angel. Near the end of the story an initially-thought innocent young boy was killed by the angel. When Moses witnessed this, Moses became upset and distrustful of the angel, until the angel, just before he made Moses leave his presence, explained to Moses how God works.

People teach that one has to go through Jesus to get to God, people bow down and pray to the cross, and even wear crosses around their necks. Thus, the only logical response is as follows: "Thou shalt have no gods before me. Thou shalt not make unto thee any graven image, or any likeness of anything that is in heaven above, or that is in the earth beneath, or that is in the water under the earth: Thou shalt not bow down thyself to them, nor serve them: for I the LORD thy God am a jealous God, visiting the iniquity of the fathers upon the children unto the third and fourth generation of them that hate me; And showing mercy unto thousands of them that love me, and keep my commandments" (Holy Bible, Exodus 20:5). Furthermore, God warns what will happen to a disobedient child, and also, what will happen to anyone who transgresses the law. For example, the child who is constantly told not to play in the streets, and the drunkard who is continually warned about speeding down neighborhood streets, will one day meet in the middle of the streets, and it won't be a pretty sight. Yes, they will cross each other out: one will go to jail, and one will go to hell. It doesn't matter whether it's John's son, or Paul's daughter, a disobedient child does not live half its days. Are you not responsible for a child, until that child reaches a certain age. How many times have you seen adults disrespected by children, and the child's parents thought it was cute? Isn't this horrible? The child is placed in the care of its parents, and if the parents allow something bad to happen to the child, it is their faults, not God's. Is this so difficult to believe?

If you were driving your car (a man made instrument), and for no apparent reason, the car quit and coasted to the side of the road, but when you got out and raised the hood, you could not determine why it stopped. Nevertheless, the vehicle would not restart. Many of your friends stopped and also looked under your hood, and each of them said, "there is no reason why your car quit, there is nothing whatsoever wrong with it! Would you believe that? Of course you would not! Your friends might not know what is wrong with the vehicle, but it is highly apparent that something is wrong with it, simply because it will not start. If all of the components are there, and all of the parts are operable, it should start! So, either all of the parts are not there, or all of the parts are not working properly. Likewise, if a person dies, his or her friends might not know what caused his or her death or his or her murder, but the reasons do exist. Autopsies reveal the causes of deaths: an autopsy which reveals lung cancer might entice one to believe that the deceased person was a heavy smoker; an autopsy which revealed a hardening of the liver, might entice one to believe that the deceased person was a heavy drinker, and so on. If one lived in a neighborhood where there were constant drive-by shootings, why would one let their children play in the yard or play on the porch? If one is not planning to steal, why would one travel with thieves? If one is not planning to commit murder, why would one travel with murderers?

Confucianism teaches that a wise man, if he can, leaves the scene, at the first moment that there is a sign of danger. What is suppose to happen to an unborn baby, when the pregnant mother uses powerful drugs like there is no tomorrow or drinks herself into a frenzy every day throughout her pregnancy? What is supposed to happen when parents allow their children to play in the streets or allow their children to run in gangs, steal, cheat others, destroy the property of others, etc.? Nevertheless, people want to believe that when a person is born blind, born deaf, or born deformed or afflicted, no one is at fault. How ironic or totally naive can an educated adult be? The parent might not know what caused it, or might not admit what caused it, but believe it, nothing evil happens from purely righteous behavior. If one believes otherwise, one does not trust God, or one does not believe in God! Don't be one of these people, Black, Brown, Red, Yellow, and White brothers and sisters. Leave these death teachings, and "Come To Life?

Because the Pentateuch (first five books), including the laws of the Bible were revealed to Moses in Africa, and the other parts revealed to God's judges, kings, major prophets, and minor prophets, with the trials and tribulations of Moses in mind, the Old Testament will be used to convince the reader that all members of mankind were meant to live as long as those individuals remained one with God. However, the New Testament will not be used, because interpretations of the New Testament seem to teach people that they have to die; that there is a heaven beyond the grave; and that they should bear the cross of Jesus the Christ, who God meant to die, regardless of how righteous Jesus remained! However, the New Testament itself could be used as effectively, because in many places the New Testament teaches that man can live forever (e.g., John 8:51, John 11:26, 1 Corinthians 3:16-17, etc.)

The ancient Egyptian (The Copts) considered everything that caused sickness, aging, or death as evil, and they shunned these things, and vice versa, they considered everything that caused health and happiness, a youthful appearance, and long life as good, and they worshipped these things.

"The Gospel According To Thomas," written in the Coptic language, a book nearly 2,000 years old, says in Log 14-16: 26-30 (p. 11) "When you see him who was not born of woman, prostrate yourselves upon your face and adore Him: He is your Father." Ironically, this is Jesus Speaking.

In the Book of Jasher, a book written during Moses's time, a book thought to have been left out of the Bible, because the Book of Jasher was confiscated by the Babylonian King, during the Babylonian captivity and never returned; it states in the first chapter, in verse ten and eleven, "And the ether brought forth every winged fowl, after its kind. And when all these things were fulfilled, behold, Jehovah appeared in Eden, and created man, and made him to be an image of his eternity."

The great ornament of the court of Charlemagne, the founder of the University of Paris, in 800, Flaccus Albinus Alcuinus, of Britain, Abbot of Canterbury, traveled throughout the Holy Land, and into the province of Persia, in search of holy things, and to see the wonders of the East. To make a long story short, Alcuin, during his nearly four year pilgrimage, stumbled upon an ascetic who told him of a Hebrew manuscript mentioned in the Books of Moses (Joshua 10:13; 2 Samuel 1:18), that had been in Persia for almost a thousand years, since the Babylonian Captivity. After, bribes consisting of pounds of gold, and hours of begging; Alcuin, after locating its whereabouts, was finally allowed to the see the Book of Jasher, kept in a locked chest, in an ancient library. Jasher was a friend of Moses himself, and witnessed with his own eyes, the events concerning Pharaoh and Moses. The reader is asked to find this book in his or her university library, and read it, and see. You will be amazed?

Who can deny, after reading the story of Adam and Eve in the Holy Bible, as well, that, Adam and Eve were going to live forever, physically, before they transgressed God's commandment and went against God? They were created to live forever, right? Most people are afraid to admit this, because it makes them responsible for their own actions, and they are not allowed to blame their evil behaviors on someone else, or to place their sins on the back of another.

After God created human beings and animals, in Genesis 1:29-39, what did God tell them to eat? "Behold, I have given you every herb bearing seed, which is upon the face of all the earth, and every tree, in the, which is a fruit of a tree yielding seed; to you it shall be for meat." "And to ever beast of the earth, and to every fowl of the air, and to every thing that creepeth upon the earth, wherein there is life, I have given every green herb for meat, and it was so." Now, who follows this commandment? Were humans meant to eat meat? Who says this, the evolutionists (who teach that man began as a cave man, forgetting their own teachings of the metamorphic stages of the human being)? The Holy Bible teaches that, "the wolf and the lamb shall feed together, and the lion shall eat straw like the bullock: and dust shall be the serpent's meat" (Isaiah 65:25). This is repeated, apparently to avoid the suspicion that this might have been a typographical error, "the wolf also will dwell with the lamb, and the leopard shall lie down with the kid" (Isaiah 11:6), "and the lion shall eat straw like and ox" (Isaiah 11:7). Will animals pave the way ffor human beings, and become vegetarians before humans do? Will, the lamb and the kid lie down with the wolf and the leopard, if the wolf and the leopard have lamb chops and goat steaks on their breaths? Is the lion merely eating straw as a salad before his meal of meat, or does the reader agree that, at this point, the animals have indeed returned to vegetarianism?

"But of the fruit of the tree (Genesis 3:3) which is in the midst of the garden, God hath said, ye shall not eat of it, neither shall ye touch it, lest ye die." If the man and the woman was going to die anyway, why would God tell them, that they would die if they ate of its fruit or die if they even touched it?

Many seminaries teach, and many scholars believe that once Adam and Eve ate of the tree, they were so sick and were suffering so greatly that God had to sacrifice two lambs and feed it to them to rid their bodies of the poison. However, when the lamb's blood entered their bodies, they were lowered away from their previous immortal and godly state to a mortal and carnal state of being, thus having a life span. This is probably the origin of the belief concerning the shedding of the blood of the lamb. This is where the coats of skin came from in Genesis (3:21).

After Adam and Eve had taken of the tree of the knowledge of good and evil, the Lord God said, "Behold the man has become as one of us, to know good and evil: and now, lest he put forth his hand, and take also of the tree of life, and eat, and live for ever; therefore, the Lord God sent him forth from the garden of Eden" (Genesis 3:21:22). Even after the man and woman had disobeyed God, as long as they were in the garden, near enough to the tree of life to take of it, they could have regained immortality, and apparently, this time, without restriction or end. And in the following verse (Genesis 3:24), Cherubims and a flaming sword were placed at the entrance of the garden to keep the way of the tree of life. Here as well, it is explained clearly to the reader that, men and women, anytime in their life, can take of the tree of life, and immortality will be theirs.

There is believed to have been approximately sixteen hundred and fifty years (1650) elapsing between the forming of Adam and Eve and the "Great Flood" of Noah's time. A couple of scores less than sixteen hundred and fifty years of eating the flesh of animals had gone on before the flood. Of course the reader is aware that Cain grew vegetables and Able raised sheep, so some have always clung to vegetarianism. Nevertheless, by Genesis 6:3, the Lord said, "My spirit shall not always strive with man, for that he also is flesh, yet his days shall be a hundred and twenty." Isn't this a big jump from Adam who lived nine hundred and thirty years, himself, and now man is given one hundred and twenty years, as a whole human race?

The new world, of course, is what scientist today refer to as the day of the caveman, because that is exactly what Noah and his sons were: cavemen, much more recent than billions of years ago. Some people cannot conceive this, they believe Noah and his sons had trailer homes on the ark, and when it landed, Noah started the first trailer park, or something to that effect. Many say that the Great Flood, in the Bible, is symbolic. Why then does the Bible give specific dimensions or exact measurements of the Boat (Holy Bible, Genesis 15 and 16)? According to the Bible, however, Noah was beginning all over, from scratch, with nothing but primitive tools, and more than likely had to hold up in the caves and hillsides of Mount Ararat, in Northeast Turkey, where the ark settled, as the first cave men and women.

Howbeit, man had now sank to the level of the beast, and everything that moved was eaten by him; and although, God had now given him everything that moveth to eat, those beast, every one, would be the cause of his death, and would also cause him to prey upon one another (Genesis 9:5).

Who has truly abided by Proverbs 4:13-27, and had some type of major problem? "And unto this people thou shalt say, Thus saith the Lord; Behold, I set before you the way of life and the way of death" (Jeremiah 21:8). Moreover, "I will punish you according to the fruit of your doings, saith the Lord," Jeremiah (21:14). Read the Wisdom of Solomon of the Catholic Bible (Chapter 1:12-16). ***Do not invite death by the error of your life, nor bring on destruction by the*** *works of your hands; because God did not make death, and he does not delight in the death of the living. For he created all things that they might exist, and the generative forces of the world are wholesome, and there is no destructive poison in them; and the dominion of Hades is not on earth. For righteousness is immortal. But ungodly men, by there words and deeds, summoned death; considering him a friend, they pined away, and they made a covenant with him, because they are fit to belong to his party."*

In the first chapter, it plainly says that God did not make death, but that man created death through the errors of his ways. This is another necessary book that the Protestants conveniently left out of their Holy Bible. "For whoso findeth me findeth life, and shall obtain favour of the Lord. But he that sinneth against me wrongeth his own soul: all they that hate me love death" (Holy Bible, Proverbs 8: 32-36). "What do you mean when you say, the fathers have eaten sour grapes and set the children's teeth on edge, all souls are mine, saith the Lord, the soul that sinneth, it shall die" (Holy Bible, Ezekiel 18:1-4) The soul is the body, contrary to what many people have been led to believe. "The Lord God formed man from the dust of the ground, and breathed into his nostrils the breath of life, and man became a living soul" (Genesis 2:7). The soul should not be confused with the spirit.

There is no book and chapter more clear about the Bible's teaching that man can live forever, in the flesh, than the book of Ezekiel chapter eighteen Please read this chapter in its entirety. It says if a man does what is lawful and right, he shall not die, and vice versa, if a man does what is wicked, in his sin that he hath sinneth, he shall die, he shall not continue to live. It says, if you do that which is right, why will you die? It says God has no pleasure in the death of anyone who dies. What is more plain than this? Have not readers of the Bible learned yet that, faith without works is dead? A plague like AIDS is very horrible; will it take the first-born of every living being to perish at once, before man begins to listen to fate? Does the world need another "Moses?"

Nevertheless, after examining other major religions of the world, merely superficially, to anyone, it should be obvious that the purposes of all God's prophets were to bring life and to bring it more abundantly, or at least to make life more enjoyable, by teaching people to be peaceful and to love one another as they love themselves. It should be equally as obvious that major religions of the world have been greatly influenced by the ancient Kamitic people of Egypt.

The Osirian history or myth, like the history or myth of Jesus, Muhammad, Buddha, Moses, Confucius, and Krishna (Vishnu), has undergone many serious changes and is told in many different ways. The most reliable accounts of Osiris, Isis, and Horus, though, might be told by the Honorable Albert Pike, Sir E. A. Wallis Budge, Manly P. Hall, Joseph Campbell, Flaccus Albinus Alcuinus, and Cyril Aldred, all of whom seem to be very thorough and extremely objective in their writings. These men should be commended most highly for their hard work toward preserving that which otherwise might have been lost forever.

Osiris, Isis, the Elder Horus, Typhon (Set) and Nephthys were the five children of the goddess Nut, the Egyptian Gods to whom the five additional days of the year are attributed. Egypt, of course emerged after the Great Flood of Noah, Ham being one of the sons of Noah. Almost all people had, of course, sunk to the level of heathens, scores of years before the flood. Nevertheless, it seems that Ham was adopted by Enoch, making Ham the first nation to become thoroughly civilized after the flood. Enoch was the father of Methuselah, the only man who walked with God and knew God's actual name. Enoch, also known as Mercury, Thoth, and Hermes, it seems, was the father of Osiris and Isis. Many believe that this is why Isis and Osiris were so wise and so powerful, and why brother and sister ruled over Egypt as husband and wife up until Cleopatra and her husband.

Christian writers will have you believe, though, that Cleopatra was from Persia or some place in that region, but was not African. Maybe this is done, because Cleopatra was said to have been the most beautiful woman who ever lived. Just like many other beautiful women, though, who delight in others' constant admiration of their unusual beauty, Cleopatra was said to have been a whore, and was very promiscuous, for which her brother, her husband, kicked her out of Egypt. Having previously traveled to Europe with her husband, and having met Julius Caesar, flirting with him every time her husband turned his back, Cleopatra knew she could find refuge in Caesar's country, or better yet, in his bed. Cleopatra finished selling her country out, to be place on the throne of Egypt, 200 years before the complete Coptic language and religion was totally discontinued, but historians of today will eagerly tell African Americans, "you know it was a black man who sold Blacks into slavery." What do you expect them to say, "The Egyptians opened their arms to Europe; educated Europeans in their best schools and universities; taught Europeans medicine to keep Europe alive; drilled Europe in the science of agriculture, and when barren European soils failed to produce adequate crops; Egyptians provided badly needed food to Europe, so that Europeans could survive its harsh winters. However, though, as soon as the opportunity presented itself; Europeans conspired with a declared lawbreaker of Egypt (Cleopatra), sneaked into the Egyptian male's bedroom, placed him in chains and placed that declared lawbreaker on the throne of Egypt to rule over Egypt: a country and a people responsible for Europe and its people being alive today!" Is this what you expect European American historians to tell you? No, they want you to believe the former, seemingly because this keeps people of color from trusting each other, keeps people of color at each other's throats, and, of course, keeps any evil reflections off the European.

The fact is that Africa was conquered, through wars, because it trusted other countries that meant it no good. No disrespect to Alex Haley, but it was obvious that the Kunta Kinte story, however good, was only superficially historically true; besides, most of the historical contents of the story, had been told on college and university campuses throughout California and other academic states, years before the made-for-television saga called "Roots" emerged. The fact is, Africa has been conquered by many countries, Greece, Rome, Arabia, and others. Many believe that "Africa" is an ancient word which means "to be afraid" or "a fearful people," named such by and after the Afrikaners or Africanus, a Roman Soldier after Hannibal. Nevertheless, conquerors always insist that the conquered people learn their customs, their religion, and, of course, their languages. What other language was Egypt to speak, when the Coptic language ceased 200 years after Cleopatra took over Egypt. The Jews could talk to Pontius Pilate almost as well as they could each other. The same as the vicious Antiochal Kings demanded that the Semitic people learn their languages.

How is it that the slaves in early American history learned to speak English, enough to talk to their slave-masters in a matter of a few months, but Africans never learned the languages of their oppressors? In learning Islam, one must learn a large portion of Arabic, and Arabia was one of the last conquerors of Africa. Still, Alex Haley presented a scenario as though Africans were like many small herds of ignorant cattle, living in many innocent little corners of the great, open-to-anyone-who-wants-anything-out-of-it, jungles of Africa. Then, the Europeans could just coast up to the shores of Africa in their slave ships, jump off the deck with nets, run down as many loose men, women, and children as his boats could hold, without even the slightest fear of altercation, and just sail right back away with a load of human cargo, not even considering for a moment that the cargo was indeed human beings. This man was not even afraid of being killed. This could only be done with the collaboration of the Arabic government or whatever government was over Africa at this time. If not, surely war and/or slaughter of many Europeans would have been inevitable.

Alex Haley, like all others, never showed anything that the Africans had ever done to or for the Europeans. Maybe young African Americans would have accepted this story and others like it less violently, if Alex Haley and others would have, first, told of Hannibal and what he did to Italy; the Jews who were enslaved by Africa for four hundred years; the Moorish Muslim conquerors from Morocco, Africa who killed, raped, and tortured both European men, women, and children and governed them for nearly seven hundred years; and other accounts in history where African people enslaved and brutalized European peoples. Tell of Russia, its domination by external Islamic forces, and their enslavement by these forces. Alex Haley and other's depictions are always as though African peoples had never had any dealings with European people before, concerning anything. Now, this is roughly 1700 years A.D., and some of the slaves, according to Alex Haley, were Muslims. Wouldn't the reader agree that this is getting pretty close to the "civilized parts of Africa?"

Unless there was a total conspiracy between governments of Europe and Africa, this depiction of what acquiring slaves was all about would have resulted in a war between countries. This war would have been similar to the wars that Alex Haley, and others who have written about slavery, so conveniently left out. Why? Are Europeans ashamed to talk about wars where European men were hung and castrated; where European women were raped and tortured; and where European men, women, and children were forced to work just to stay alive, or does it just make Europeans angry and beligerent, and this is an area that others dare not tread? Why does anyone not talk about why Italians have brown eyes and black hair, why Greeks have brown eyes and black hair, especially why people in Spain have brown eyes and black hair, and why Pharaoh is depicted as being solely responsible for enslaving the Jews during Moses' time, instead of Jews, in reality, were enslaved by Africans? Is it beginning to look more like pay-back or retaliation, now? Imagine an injustice that was so cruel and so embarrassing that the victim had to get pay-back from the perpetrator, but the victim could not allow anyone (especially the perpetrator) to know what the pay-back was all about; because it was so disgusting and so demeaning. Nevertheless if, indeed, this can be imagined; the situation with African slavery can be easily understood, in its entirety.

In realizing a dire need to conclude this particular segment, a short story has come to mind that the reader must hear. Two African American males were arguing about the age one has to be, if one desired to become a Christian minister. One was claiming to be a minister, and the other was inquiring as to his age. The former said he was thirty-one years old, and the latter was calling him a liar, saying that he was not old enough to be a minister, that he was far too young. All the time the argument was going on, about the span of about fifteen minutes, a Caucasian male was standing nearby listening to the argument. Finally, the Caucasian interrupted and said, "I'm a minister." The African American gentleman who had been insisting that thirty-one years old was far too young of an age, for a person to be a minister, quickly asked, "oh yeah, how old are you?" The Caucasian gentleman responded, "twenty-seven." The African American gentleman, who had been so viciously calling the other African American gentleman a liar for insisting he was a minister at the age of thirty-one, merely responded humbly by asking, "You is?" Now this is what he said verbatim, no argument at all. "You is, not you are, you is!" However, he was giving the African American gentleman pure unadulterated hell, for claiming to be a minister at the age of thirty-one.

The point is that Blacks will allow Whites to be anything they want to be, and will believe anything they say, and will allow Whites to discredit Blacks, without even giving that Black a chance or without even researching what that Black has said. Does the reader follow what is being said concerning this behavior of African Americans toward each other? This true story needed to have been told, because many will attempt to discredit this book, for no other reason than the fact that it has been written by a non-European, both Blacks and Whites. Nevertheless, the author asks the reader to read it, and afterwards, ask your friends and loved ones to read it, and leave those death teachings of traditional Christianity, traditional Islam, traditional Hinduism, and other religions that teach its followers that they were born to die, and "Come To Life and Live Forever in the Flesh!"

COPTIC MIXTURE

Ⲁⲗ	Bв	Гг	Ⲇⲗ	Єϵ	Ⲋ	Ⲍⲍ	Ηн	Θθ	Iι	Κк
alpha	vesta	ghamma	delta	ei	soo	zeta	eeta	theeta	iota	kappa
a	b, v	g, gh, ng	th, d	e	6	z	ee	th, t	i, y	k
[a]	[b, v]	[g, ɣ]	[ð, d]	[ɛ, e]		[z]	[t]	[θ]	[ɪ, i]	[k]

Ⲗⲗ	Ⳙⲙ	Ⲛⲛ	Ⲝⲝ	Oo	Ⲡπ	Pρ	Cc	Ⲧⲧ	Ⲩⲩ	Φφ
lamda	mai	nai	eksee	o	pee	ro	seema	tav	epsilon	fei
l	m	n	x	o (short)	p	r	s	t, d	v, u, y	f
[l]	[m]	[n]	[ks]	[ɔ]	[p]	[r]	[s]	[t, d]	[v, u, ɪ]	[f]

Ⲭⲭ	Ⲯⲯ	Ⲱⲱ	Ⳳϣ	Ϥϥ	Ϧϧ	Ϩϩ	Ϫϫ	Ϯ	Ϫⲍ
kai	epsee	o	shai	fai	khai	horee	theema	tee	janja	jinkim
k, sh, kh	ps	o (long)	sh	f	kh	h	ch	tee	g, j
[k, ∫x]	[ps]	[ɔː]	[∫]	[f]	[x]	[h]	[ʧ]	[ti]	[g ʤ]

THE SIGNIFICANCE OF LANGUAGE

Many Americans, who are obviously of African-related descent, consider themselves as African-Americans, but some of them are afraid to identify with Africa? Is it logical to consider oneself European-American, and be afraid to study European culture, European history, and the origins of European religions, etc.?

Many European-Americans are proud to say they can speak German, Spanish, or French, and many are proud to say they have visited Spain, Germany, or France. Should African-Americans continue, throughout eternity, to be ashamed to identify with Africa, ashamed to say they may have been Coptic, and that they could very well have been that very same Egyptian of ancient Egypt, but, indeed, should people of color be afraid to say that they may be of African-related descent?

African Americans, more than anyone else, seemingly, are constantly reminded that they know no other language, other than the languages of their conquerors, or their ex-slave-masters. A very good example is Spanish-speaking people originating from the Americas. How often, does the reader remember, having been in crowded elevators, on crowded streets, or in stores, when people who are non-English-speaking are nearby (e.g., Arabs, Mexicans, Orientals, etc.) and all of a sudden, they began speaking their language, seemingly, as loudly as they possibly could? Why does the reader suppose this is done? Nothing positive seems to come to mind, does it?

Nevertheless, this book is to remind you, or to help you realize how totally ignorant some people truly are. For example, some Spanish Americans (i.e., Mexicans, Chicanos, Cubans, etc.) will so hastily say to African Americans, "at least I have my own country," forgetting that scores of them are being caught, raped, murdered, beaten, and arrested daily, attempting to flee "their country" to this one, that African Americans help build, for a more human way of life. Moreover, this language (Spanish), that Spanish Americans call their very own, belongs to none other than their conquerors: the Spaniards. Furthermore, from most of their appearances, they took on, not only, the Spaniard's language in its entirety, losing the language of their forefathers, altogether, but their race was raped beyond recognition. They look more like the Spaniard than they do themselves, and they have the audacity to mock African Americans and European Americans with the Spaniard's language. How ignorant can some adults allow themselves to be? Mexican Americans and African Americans have experienced the same horrible histories.

All throughout Central and South America, many inhabitants of the land speak Spanish and French. Are they Spaniards and Frenchmen? Of course not! Do they know this? Well, many of them certainly don't act like it, do they? Fortunately, this behavior is about to come to an end, because, now, they are asked to forget Spanish and take on the language of the Englishmen. Can this be done? Can a people be asked to stop speaking their own language?

Culture can basically be summed up in one word: Language. One's language is the origin and the total embodiment of one's culture. Language, not only, restores one's culture, but restores one's history of oneself.

Why must a people continually depend solely on the languages of others? Why must a people continue to worship messengers, prophets, and gods who look like people other than themselves? Why is it considered deviant behavior, when a people strive to identify with their ancestors, the gods and religions of their ancestors, and the language of their ancestors? Most importantly, though, is the question, "does a race of people really care about another race of people, when they do not want for that race of people, what they so forcefully want for themselves?"

A complete language only consists of about 1200 words. Actually, because of the existence, now, of so many synonyms and so much technological jargon, a language can actually be complete, being comprised of approximately 700-900 words. Does the reader know anyone or know of anyone who uses 900 different words, in normal everyday conversation? Who does this in the span of a week or even a month? What about in a year?

Finally, at the end of 1996, America resorted to the most current issue involving "Black English." How demeaning and condescending can one race be to another? Ebonics, what insults will America resort to next. African Americans can speak any language anyone else can speak and can do anything anyone else can do. When will non-African Americans learn that African Americans, from birth, learn to resist English? They learn not to want to speak the languages of European Americans, because of what they have been taught that European Americans have done to them, and of course, because of the racial discrimination and physical abuse they have witnessed themselves.

However, when African Americans come to realize that this language called English has undergone so many changes, since its origin in Africa, they will feel more comfortable about speaking it. The languages are so similar that English seems merely a derivative of the Coptic language.

European Americans say "Haht Dahg," African Americans say Haht Dawg. European Americans say "Lahg and Frahg," African Americans say "Lawg and Frawg." Neither is saying "Hot Dog, Log, or Frog," which are all pronounced with O sounds. The European Americans resist the short vowel system, because it was imposed upon them by the East, or by their Afro-Asiatic conquerors, and African Americans resist what they have been forced to believe is English, because they believe it is the language of their oppressors, or their English-speaking conquerors.

African Americans should know that the Greeks got much of their Greek language from the Copts or Egyptians, through people like Aristotle, Plato, and Alexander, the son of Philip. Italy was deeply influence by Hannibal, from Carthage, Africa. Spain was deeply influenced by the Moors (Muslims) from Morocco, Africa. So, then, where did Europeans get their language? Yes, from the Coptic language of the ancient Egyptians of North Eastern Africa!

If African Americans can sing English just as well as their European counterparts, they can speak it just as well, believe this, if the reader believes nothing else said in this book. Most African Americans go out of their ways not to look or act European or "White," just as many European American go out of their ways not to look "Black." The brilliant Jawanza Kunjufu might say, "If acting "White" is acting good or proper, then what is acting "Black." This makes sense, but Jawanza must admit that a distinction can be made between the physical attributes of Blacks and Whites, as well as the differences between their physical mannerisms.

European Americans approach to many things they do physically is much different than that of Blacks, whether good or bad, better or worst. Females are softer than males, but this does not make them inferior! Kung-fu is softer than most styles of martial arts, but is believed to be equal and, in some cases, superior to harder styles. Likewise, if one did not know how brilliant and superbly educated, indeed, Jawanza Kunjufu is, by simply listening to his "country or southern" dialect, one would think he was uneducated. Jawanza Kunjufu sounds like he's from the deep south or uneducated. Many Blacks would refer to the way Jawanza talks as "country." Moreover, some so-called African Americans can stand behind a partition and speak, and one would swear it was an American-born Caucasian, but if Jawanza Kunjufu stood behind a partition and spoke, almost all Americans would guess that he was not Caucasian. The same goes for Martin Luther King, Malcolm X, Louis Farrakhan, Maya Angelou, Nikki Giovanni, James Baldwin, and others who have become well-educated, and who spoke or who speaks with magnificent clarity, but have maintained their cultures. On the other hand, Allan Keyes is a very intelligent and very educated "BLACK" man, but if he was standing behind a partition while speaking, one might mistake him for an American born Caucasian, he speaks the American English language very fluently and with a European American accent.

American English is the only language in the world that is built around a new and distinguished, supposedly, long vowel system. All other languages use a very traditional short vowel system, as the basis of their means of pronunciation. A huge portion of American English is borrowed from other languages, which is usually very distinguishable, simply because the words are usually pronounced with short vowels (e.g., father as opposed to lather).

The English spoken in England and Great Britain is spoken with the short vowel pronunciation. The Europeans who settled in this country, the country we now call America, resisted the King's English, the same as African Americans and other oppressed minorities resist American English today; nevertheless, the result of this resistance of the King's English, and various contributions from other cultures, is known today as American English: the new long vowel system.

Whenever a word is spoken with short (a) sound or a short (I) sound, it is purely debatable whether that word is a word of American origin. The word usually has a foreign origin. Words created or founded in America, by Europeans, usually have the American English pronunciation. That is, they are usually spoken using the Long Vowel sounds.

However, there are always exceptions to every rule, but overall, the words will follow a standard method of being pronounced, if they are considered to be of American origin, by Europeans. This distinguishes American English words from even those of words from England.

The alphabets of the Coptic language, and there values can be seen on the significance of language chart image or in any Coptic Language manuscript.

It doesn't take a mathematical genius or a rocket scientist to see that the first two letters in the Coptic language are ALPHA and BIDA. The Greeks took the letters and changed the names of some of them. They call their first two letters ALPHA and BETA.

Now, the Caucasian or European American calls the first two letters of the American English alphabet A and B, but refer to all of them as the ALPHA-BET. How amazingly similar the word Alphabet is to Alpha Beta, and how amazingly similar Alpha Beta is to Alpha Bida. Are you finally getting the picture? If this is not true, where does the reader think the letters used in American English came from? Yes, English alphabets came from the Greeks, and the Greek alphabet came from the Copts. Thus the question reemerges: Should African Americans continue to be apprehensive in speaking English, thinking that American English belongs exclusively to Caucasian Americans?

It seems English belongs to African Americans as much as it does anyone else, simply because, the origin of all occidental languages seem to be made up primarily of Coptic letters, numbers, and words.   Remember, AH, AY, EE, OH, OO, not A, E, I , O, U, okay? Americans even use Arabic numerals!

It has been taught that the first man who learned the science of counting or mathematics was a shepherd who taught himself to keep a rock for every sheep in his flock and a second bag to transfer to and from. If he had a rock left in the bag he was transferring from, he knew he had lost a sheep. It was said that he became so fond of the rocks, he named them. Guess what he named the first three rocks? Yes, in English, the names would be, one, two, and three. After a few years he did not need the rocks at all.

The world has advanced very much since this shepherd and since the ancient Egyptians. The ancient Egyptians made a mark for each number. After making ten marks, they began using symbols to represent the number ten, the number one hundred, five hundred, one thousand, ten thousand, one million, one billion and so on.

Once Egypt was betrayed and conquered, there language and counting system that had been shared with the rest of the known world eventually became obsolete. The Arabic numerals replaced the Egyptian numerals, just as Arabic words and terms replaced many Egyptian terms. However, the Egyptian's true system of science, religion, and mathematics died with the ancient Egyptian. This has been discovered by modern day mathematicians who have attempted to study the pyramids, the sphinx, and the many other wonders of ancient Egypt.

Therefore, the numeric system shared by the Egyptians with the rest of the known world is outdated and has been surpassed by modern day systems.

NORTH TO SOUTH

WHY SO MANY AMAZING RELIGIONS?

Religion, up to now, has merely served humankind in helping people accept death, without going insane before actually dying. If people thought they would die and would never come back to this earth, nor would they ever live again in any other form anywhere; people would panic when they came near to death, and there is no telling what each person might do just before he or she died. Religion, though, helps to ease a person's fear, by promising an eternal salvation for that person's soul, if that person has followed a certain code of righteous conduct or behavior, during that person's life.

Each religion has a set of stories concerning various "God-Sent and God-Fearing Men and Women" and how they conquered the evils of the world and how they taught others to conquer themselves and eventually the evils around them. These stories and the many parables used throughout these stories inspire people to be faithful and forbearing. Other stories of saints, prophets, and saviors entering a beautiful paradise where there is no pain and suffering and somehow leaving descriptions of and directions to that paradise has prompted a huge percentage of the good behavior you see in people, just as stories of sinners entering fiery infernos; stories of sinners suffering many horrible types of deaths and misfortunes; and the promises that sinners will awaken from death one day, to be condemned to suffer for eternity, has kept people from being all out sinners while they are in their primes, and then freaking out and killing every one they hate just before they die, or just before they commit suicide.

Just imagine what the world would be like if there was no religion, if there was nothing written telling a person how one should treat another, and if a person could do anything he or she wanted to do. What if people believed there was no God, and they believed that people should live like the lions, the tigers, and the other wild animals of the jungle. If a person could run another down and take his or her belongings, then it belongs to them now; and if a person was strong enough to snatch another out of his or her vehicle, then the vehicle should belong to them. Is this the way people should live, and then should they be taught that after a life of this type of behavior, they simply die, fade away, and will be no more? It is not unbearable yet! Less than five percent (5%) of society is considered criminal. Imagine if crime was multiplied by ten, and fifty percent (50%) of humanity became criminal. Imagine if half of the people (50%) went out every day purposely to commit some type of crime? Do you realize that criminals would only have one person each to prey upon? This would not be a very healthy society at all; people would not be safe even looking out of windows in their own homes.

However, should religion do more than just ease the agony of accepting an ever approaching death? If a person spends, literally, a lifetime doing good and making life pleasant for others, shouldn't that person have a special gift reserved for him or her that would guarantee that person, for eternity, the same as that person had tried to give others? Should that person have to leave this earth to receive this gift? No, of course not! Why should they? God is not hidden from people. Is the sun hanging from a string, or is it just there? Are the heavenly bodies that we refer to as stars all hanging from strings, or are they just there with nothing holding them up? God is not hidden! When something bad happens to a person, is it because this person was a nice guy or because this person was a fool? Some people want to hear voices coming out of the clouds, in order to believe in God; they have never once considered that they don't have extension cords running from their bodies to outlets in the walls, and that they don't have twelve volt batteries stored in their chests. Some people are so hung up on a story of a man with long white hair and a staff, up in the clouds, sitting on a throne; and the story of a red man with horns, tail, and a pitchfork, living in a fiery furnace; until, it is almost impossible for them to believe in a God who is closer to them than their juggler vein! Every major religious text teaches of that God (the one who is closer than one's juggler vein), regardless of what the people's interpretations might be, believe it or not!

When thinking about, writing about, and/or talking about religion, people rarely consider the many similarities in different religions; especially, when examining the definition and the origin of religion. People would rather, though, consider the few differences in religion, and have succeeded in associating different peoples of different geographical locations with different religions, thus attempting to keep themselves divided. All Americans are supposed to be Christians; all Arabians are supposed to be Muslim; all Chinese are supposed to be Buddhist, Confucian, or Taoist, etc.; and all Indians are supposed to be Hindus, etc. However, each religion has the golden rule, "Do unto others as you will have others do unto you." Isn't this strange?

Why can't people just consider the fact that God's word has been sent to many people in many languages, and that if God is a fair God, God loves all races equally? If, indeed, this is true, why would God give Europeans the truth, and then turn around and tell all the other races a bald faced lie? Shame on God! Would God do this, or would God give all races the truth in their own languages? The truth can be made manifest in many forms as well as a lie can be made manifest in many forms. Besides, which is most important: (1) the race of the characters in a story, or (2) the story itself? Most level headed people in America would probably choose number two, and some might even admit that it really doesn't matter what the color or race was of Jesus, himself, but then why has it been such a desperate attempt to get the world to see Jesus as a white person. Perhaps it does matter to some people that Jesus be thought of as White. It just brings about the question, "Why would one teach that a person is a Jew (Hebrew), dark-skinned, from Northeast Africa (who looked so much like his brothers that Judas Iscariot had to kiss him, so that the Roman soldiers would know who Jesus was), and then (later), turn around and paint all pictures of Jesus showing Jesus as White, and depict Jesus in all movies, television programs, and children's books as being white with all European features?"

In America, more than anywhere else, because of the doctrine America preaches, accepting all races and cultures under one banner, a picture of the savior of all mankind should not resemble any particular race. His or her face should always be hidden behind a glowing light or something to that effect. That way everyone can accept him or her (the gender as well should not be known). Most established religions are chauvinistic to say the least; they all place the male high above the female, and all of their prophets, angels, and messiahs are all male. The ancient Egyptian culture believed in equality among genders, as Osiris and Isis were sister and brother; all other rulers over Egypt were to be brother and sister. The goal was cleanliness and life through vegetarianism and a love and respect for life and happiness for all the living. The goal and mission of King Osiris' were to spread vegetarianism and peace throughout the world.

WHY PROTEST THE

APOCRYPHA ?

Why is it that the Catholics have more books in their Bible than the Protestants or other Christians have in their Bibles? Did God tell them more than God told other believers about the same Jesus Christ? Did he talk more to Catholics than he did to other so-called Christians? Why do Protestants (Baptists, Methodists, Pentecost, etc.) have only sixty-six books in their Bibles and Catholics have an Apocrypha which contains at least seven additional books and sometimes as many as fourteen or fifteen additional books? Those books of the Apocrypha are as follows: Esdras 1; Esdras 2; Esdras 3; Esdras 4; Tobit; Judith; Additions to Esther; The Wisdom of Solomon; Sirach; Baruch; The Letter of Jeremiah; The Prayer of Azariah & Song of the Three Young Men; Susanna; Bel and the Dragon; The Prayer of Manasseh; 1 Maccabees; and 2 Maccabees.

Why would one Christian study something different or study additional books, claiming that they are part of the Holy Bible and another Christian leave those books out of their Bible and claim that those books have no place in the Holy Bible? Are those additional books filled with lies? Are Christians, other than Catholics, ashamed of those books because they are filled with truth? What could the real reasons be that Protestants neglect to consider these additional books? What is the definition of Catholic? What is the definition of Protestant? Is it coincidental that the origin of the word Protestant is protest?

The Catholic is specifically of Rome or originating in Rome (e. g., Roman Catholic); Of the ancient undivided Church; Of interest or use to all people; broad; universal; A member of the Catholic Church.

The Protestant Christian Churches which split off from the Catholic Churches during the Reformation of the 1500's, or developed thereafter, were many (e.g., Lutherans, Baptists, Presbyterians, Methodists, and Quakers, etc.).

Why did these other Churches separate? Why did the Protesters or Protestants keep some of the books but take a large number of them out? Are the Catholics claiming something that is a lie, or are the Protestants denying something that is true? Perhaps, the books that are contained in the Apocrypha, not only, cover a certain portion of history that condemns Christians, but that it also suggest a slightly different doctrine of Jesus that condemns the teachings of Protestants altogether (e. g., man created to die regardless of his works; Jesus changing God's laws to fit man; etc.) If the latter is the case, then what Protestants have done could be more serious than most minds could even imagine! Could Protestants have actually been teaching ignorant followers that they have to die, when they actually do not, if they follow the correct doctrine? Could Protestants have been teaching ignorant followers that Jesus changed God's laws, when in reality, someone else (Invaders/Oppressors of Jews) changed God's laws? This could prove to be a very serious offense against God!

Nevertheless, the Protestants must, indeed, be protesting something, and whatever it is must have something to do with the books the Protestants have chosen to leave out of their Holy Bible!

It is documented history that Alexander the Great did, in fact, exist, but the Protestants chose to omit it from their religious text! Instead, they leave a large questionable gap between their book of Malachi and their New Testament book of Matthew. Should this be acceptable, when any logical individual knows that four hundred years cannot go by without one single event occurring? Yet, the Protestants choose to have a huge gap, instead of including, at least, a little bit of rhetorical historical coverage. What, if anything, are they hiding or are ashamed of writing of themselves?

Beginning with the book of (Tobit), Raphael, one of the seven Holy Angels speaks, but even more enlightening, it states, "It is good to guard the secret of a king, but gloriously to reveal the works of God. Do good and evil will not overtake you. <u>Prayer is good when accompanied by fasting</u>, almsgiving and righteousness (Tobit 12: 8). Are Protestants afraid that someone will read this statement and conclude that prayer alone is not good enough and that they need to fast? In verse ten, it says that "those who commit sin are the enemies of their own lives," does this contradict their teaching that it is impossible not to sin?

In Judith, it states, "Do not try to bind the purposes of God; for God is not like man, to be threatened, nor like a human being, to be won over by pleading" (Judith 8: 16). Do Protestants suspect that this might stop their members from begging God for mercy and gifts, knowing they are transgressing the law and sinning throughout each day, and especially praying for God to bless someone else who they know is a devil and needs to straighten up before expecting any favors from God?

What about the book of Esther in the Protestants Holy Bible? Why does this book stop at the third verse of Chapter Ten? Why does it have no Chapter Eleven at all? Chapter Eleven mentions Cleopatra; is she so horrible to include in one's Holy Bible? Is "Cleopatra" a dirty word among Protestants? Is this not an historical character?

In the book of Sirach (2: 15), it states that "Those who fear the Lord will not disobey his words, and those who fear the Lord will seek his approval, and those who love him will be filled with the law!" Why do Protestants hate the law and feel that it is impossible to abide by? Do people have to lie, to steal, to commit adultery, to kill, to hate the Sabbath, and to dishonor their mother and father? Does this not keep an individual safe (Sirach 3: 1-16)?

The most condemning of all the books left out by Protestants is the Wisdom of Solomon! "Wisdom will not enter a deceitful soul, nor dwell in a body enslaved to sin. For a holy spirit will flee from deceit, and will rise and depart from foolish thoughts, and will be ashamed at the approach of unrighteousness" (Wisdom of Solomon: 4-5).

The most condemning of the verses in the Wisdom of Solomon states, "Do not invite death by the error of your life, nor bring on destruction by the works of your hands; because God did not make death, and he does not delight in the death of the living. For God created all things that they might exist, and the generative forces of the world are wholesome, and there is no destructive poison in them; and the dominion of Hell is not on earth, for righteousness is immortal. But ungodly men, by their words and deeds, summoned death; considering him a friend, they pined way, and they made a covenant with him, because they are fit to belong to his party" (Wisdom of Solomon 1:12-16). Protestants want you to believe that God has ordained your death, simply because you have been born!

This scripture completely contradicts the Protestants teaching that humans have to die and that man was born to die. Reader, they have been lying to you!

The following chapter explains their reasoning for practicing evil and for killing and oppressing righteous people. It is enough to make a righteous individual sick (Wisdom 2: 1-23).

There is one book in the Catholic Bible that Protestants left out of theirs that tells exactly how the Mosaic Law was changed. It has nothing to do with Jesus! This act occurred scores of years before the birth of Jesus. Yet, people teach that Jesus changed the Law of his "father." This is criminal! Jesus was not even born, when the Greeks came down from their country, into the Jordan Valley, and began to rape and murder and ultimately demand the change of their religious customs!

One of the Antiochal kings, following Alexander, came to Jerusalem with a large force. Deceitfully he spoke peaceable words to the people of Jerusalem, and they believed him; but he suddenly fell upon the city, dealt it a severe blow and destroyed many people of Israel. And they stationed there a sinful people, lawless men (1 Maccabees 1: 29-35).

Why are people teaching that Jesus is responsible for the changes in the customs of the Jews and that Jews killed Jesus?

The Antiochal king then wrote to his whole kingdom that all should be one people, and that each individual must give up his customs. And the king sent letters by messengers to Jerusalem and the cities of Judah. He directed them to follow customs strange to the land, to forbid burnt offerings in the sanctuary, to profane Sabbaths and feasts, to defile the sanctuary and the priests, to sacrifice swine and unclean animals, and to leave their sons uncircumcised. They were to make themselves abominable by everything unclean and profane, so that they should forget the law and change all the ordinances. And whoever does not obey the command of the king should die (1 Maccabees 1: 41-51). Does this sound like Jesus gave permission for some of the laws of Moses to be disobey? What are people afraid of? They say that the truth will set you free; do they not want to be free? In (2 Maccabees 7: 1-6), anyone who would refuse to eat pork was cooked him or herself in large skillets! Does this sound like Jesus allowing people to disobey some of the laws of Moses? Wake up people?

The killing thing is that Protestants have the gall to leave something like this out of their Bible, after entering so much other unnecessary filth! At least, Catholics had the nerve to tell the truth, but they still eat swine and live by this evil command given by this evil king hundreds of years ago, and they die in it. Why? Why are Catholics still teaching to die and go and live with Jesus, when they know this is not what Jesus was teaching? Is living as equals with people of color so horrible? Come To Life, People?

There is only one other reason why Catholics, after knowing the truth and printing it in their Bible, choose to live sinful lives and die in their sins. That reason it that they believe as it is written in the Wisdom of Solomon, in the second chapter:

For they reasoned unsoundly, saying to themselves, short and sorrowful is our life, and there is no remedy when a man comes to his end, and no one has been known to return from Hell.

Because we were born by mere chance, and hereafter we shall be as though we had never been; because the breath in our nostrils is smoke, and reason is a spark kindled by beating of our hearts.

When it is extinguished, the body will turn to ashes, and the spirit will dissolve like empty air. Our name will be forgotten to time, and no one will remember our works; our life will pass away like the traces of a cloud and be scattered like mist that is chased by the rays of the sun and overcome by its heat.

For our allotted time is the passing of a shadow, and there is no return from our death, because it is sealed up and no one turns back.

Come, together, therefore, let us enjoy the good things that exist, and make use of the creation to the full as in youth.....Let us oppress the righteous poor man; let us not spare the widow nor regard the gray hairs of the aged. But, let our might be our law of right, for what is weak proves itself to be useless.

Let us lie in wait for the righteous man, because he is inconvenient to us and opposes our actions....

We are considered by him as something base, and he avoids our ways as unclean; he boasts that God is his father.

Let us see if his words are true, and let us test, and let us test what will happen at the end of his life; if the righteous man is God's son, he will help him, and will deliver him from the hands of his adversaries.

Let us test him with insult and torture, that we may find out how gentle he is, and make trial of his forbearance.

Let us condemn him to a shameful death, for, according to what he says, he will be protected....

For God created man not for corruption, and made him in the image of his own eternity, but through the devil's envy, death entered into the world, and those who belong to his party experience it.

This chapter, the book of Maccabees, and the Wisdom of Solomon confirm three suspicions: (1) descendants of Greeks (Alexander) killed Jesus and knew exactly what they were doing; (2) Jews did not nor did they have the authority to kill Jesus nor any other righteous man; and (3) death is caused by man, and man is the cause, through the lack of faith, of his own dying.

It also becomes obvious that there is a great chance that some Catholics knowingly worship Alexander the Great, who did exactly as is written in the Wisdom of Solomon (Chapter 2), who was thirty-three years old when he died, the same age of death that is claimed for Jesus, and who was also called the Son of God or the Son of Zeus!

EAST TO WEST

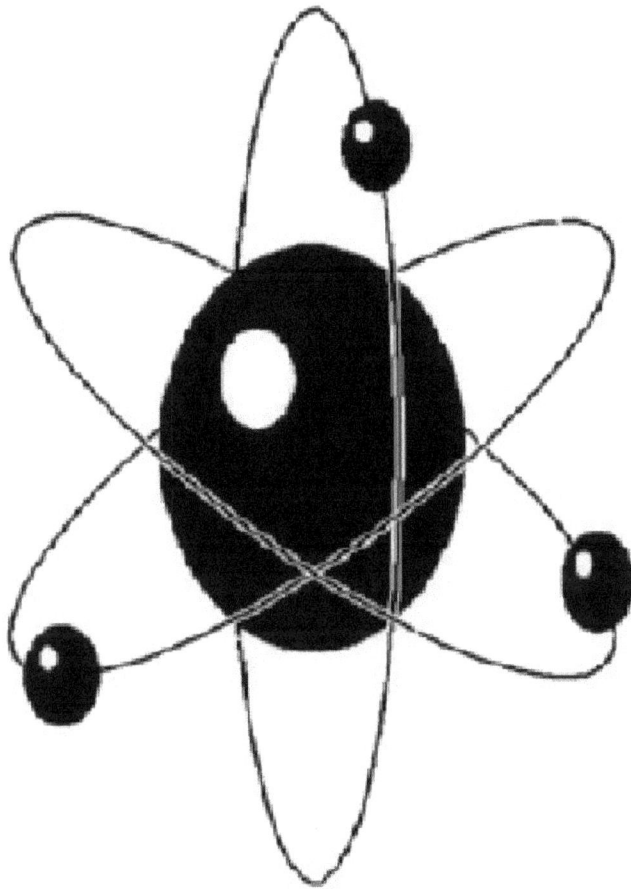

Did England Know Of India
BEFORE 1611

Hinduism can be dated back about 1500-1200 B.C.; however, some have even suggested as far back as 4000-3500 B. C. If one would count the years between the flood of Noah's time and the birth and life of Adam and Eve, one might come up with about 1651 years. From the flood to the life of Jesus one might count a little more than 2300 years. Adding the number of years between Adam and Eve of the Holy Bible and the number of years between the flood of Noah and the life and times of Jesus or Isa, one might count approximately 4000 years.

In the King James' version of the Christians' Holy Bible, in the book of Genesis, in sixteenth verse of chapter four, it states, "And Cain went out from the presence of the Lord, and dwelt in the land of Nod, on the east of Eden. And Cain knew his wife; and she conceived and bare Enoch: and he builded a city and called the name of the city after the name of his son, Enoch. And unto Enoch was born Irad: and Irad begat Mehujael: and Mehujael begat Methusael: and Methusael begat Lamech. And Lamech took unto him two wives: the name of the one was Adah, and the name of the other Zillah. And Adah bare Jabal: he was the father of such that dwell in tents, and of such as have cattle. And his brother's name was Jubal: he was the father of all such as handle the harp and organ." Now keep in mind that Cain was suggested to be a connoisseur of vegetables, while Abel was suggested to raise meats for food (Genesis 4: 2).

The Bible further suggests that Noah had three sons, from whence came Ham: the African; Shem: the Middle Easterner; and Japheth: the European, while Noah makes up the people of Ayatollah or Turkey. Life, as the inhabitants of earth know it, began in Turkey, simply because Noah's ark was halted in Mount Ararat. Mount Ararat is located in Northeast Turkey. "And the ark rested in the seventh month, on the seventeenth day of the month, upon the mountains of Ararat" (Genesis 8: 4). Surely, Noah and his crew would have to begin here, seeing as though this is where they unavoidably ended up. Now the question is, where did the people of India originate? Remember, they were not part of Noah's crew.

Is it not strange that Cain and China are so similar and that the word Nod means to bow, but is it not especially strange that Cain was vegetarian and the people of China and India are also mostly vegetarian or very closely vegetarian?

Some Bible scholars might argue, justifiably, that "the waters prevailed exceedingly upon the earth; and all the high hills, that were under the whole heaven, were covered (Genesis 7: 19). "And all flesh died that moved upon the earth, both the fowl, and of cattle, and of beast, and of every creeping thing that creepeth upon the earth, and every man died (Genesis 7: 21): All in whose nostrils was the breath of life, of all that was in the dry land, died. And every living substance was destroyed which was upon the face of the ground, both man, and cattle, and the creeping things, and the fowl of the heaven; and they were destroyed from the earth: and Noah only remained, and they that were with him in the ark (Genesis 7: 22-23).

Therefore, anyone arguing that the entire earth was covered with water is justified, "because the Bible tells them so." However, after exploring science, it is discovered that rain is no hocus pocus event or incident. Rain occurs after the sun has drawn the water from the earth into a formation of clouds, and then after the clouds become heavy enough, varying sky temperatures working with gravity causes rain. The author is no science major but understands that rain is more in the line with law than magic. The point is that the earth is three-fifths water, and even if the sun drew every single drop of all three-fifths of the earth's water into the sky, it could only rain three-fifths back to the earth. How is it possible to cover the whole earth? It could only cover three-fifths of it, and this is only if all three-fifths of the earth's water had been drawn into the sky. Does this make any kind of sense?

Another story that you may not have heard is that life began somewhere near the beginning of the Nile River, where two twin mountains emerge from the earth, and the sun can clearly be seen rising between the two huge mountains as though the sun is being born each day. Life beginning at the Nile River caused the original people to build their homes and lifestyles around the Nile River.

One individual began to build boats, and this individual sailed the Nile daily. This river runs northward into the Mediterranean Sea. After studying the Nile for many years, this individual began to suspect that it was going to flood excessively and rapidly and would kill all who lived near it and even for miles beyond its banks. This flood, he suspected, would spread for many miles, overwhelming all human life, which was then closely gathered around the Nile River. All the people thought this individual was crazy (i.e., delusional or insane). After several desperate attempts, he realized that he could not convince them of this catastrophe; therefore, he began to build a huge sailing vessel that would house many land animals and all who believed in his suspicion. Unfortunately, the only ones who believed in this individual was his family. When the rains came and the flood began, the people could not escape the flooding Nile River and they all were killed. The Nile flowing northward took the huge vessel northward into Turkey where it finally was halted far into the mountains of Ararat in Northeast Turkey, hundreds of miles away.

The point, however, is that the whole earth was not flooded, only the whole earth as those people knew it. The people (Cain's descendants) who had been exiled from that part of the land and who had traveled eastward into what is now known as China and India went unaffected by that flood.

This is the beginning of the reasons why the world has Shem, Ham, Japheth and who the world refers to as Indians and Orientals or Far Easterners.

Those people believe in long life and study vegetarianism, just as did Cain. In India, people are predominantly vegetarian; however, the country is poor, and the people eat many beans, potatoes and wheat. Those grains and starches are far too strong to be digested by mere cow's milk. Thus, the people of those countries suffer the highest rate of diabetes in the world. They did, however, predict the end of the world producing a vegetarian savior who is musically inclined and will destroy incarnate error (Lord Shiva: The Lord of Dance). The western world calls this individual Christ!

If you are just drinking milk, and no other animal products, do not eat very much starch. Garden vegetables are all that can be digested with milk alone. Most starches are too strong for the human body anyway! So, why eat them? They are for animals, and animals are of the field; man is of the garden!

However, even though the people of India might be missing the main ingredients in their diet that could prevent this amazing number of cases of diabetes resulting in death and discomfort; they still are considered by many to be the most beautiful of people. So, their diet does have a positive effect on their physical being; they just live in impoverished conditions, not excluding their population size, that prevents them from growing the vegetables necessary to escape diabetes. Their vegetables/starches are too dry and of course too starchy, and by their not eating meat, they cannot digest the starch. Thus, they get the beauty from the essence of the plant but their arteries are congested by the build-up of the starch. Therefore, they get the beauty but not the longevity to the extent that they are free from pain and discomfort. Their diet is similar to flushing newspaper or rags down a commode.

People of India are not totally exempt from derogatory rumors of their origin. Many religious discussions give birth to many weird stories. Moreover, the Bible chose not to include any logical story of how Cain could have gotten married, when there were only two boys on the whole earth with their father and mother. If it is not told who exactly he could have married; people will develop their own theories. Some people have connected the Chinese Monks, the vegetarian customs and the Mongoloid features of the people, and they have come up with the idea that Cain mated with an ape or gorilla and produced the oriental peoples of the world. Although I have heard this theory; I did not develop this theory and this is not my theory!

In the Holy Qur'an, it mentions someone being turned into apes. Elijah Muhammad taught that a community of Europeans, at one point, attempted to return to their natural features or natural self, and was turned into apes. Upon reading the Holy Qur'an in the part of the book referred to as the Cow or The Heifer , Surah 2:65, and the Heights, Surah 7:166, it mentions a community of people whose diet was mainly fish who were transformed into apes. Of course, its footnotes written in English give a different explanation. Nevertheless, it does state this idea!

In the chapter referred to as the Cave, Surah 18:18, it tells of the people who were driven into caves to live for so many years that no one knew how long they had been there. In Surah 18:25, it is said that these people resided in the caves for twelve hundred (1200) years. However, it does state that their features changed to the point that if anyone had come upon them, they surely would have run away in terror or fright. Islam teaches that Europeans were exiled into caves by Africans and other peoples of the world for many horrible things they did to others. They were said to have lived there like beasts, eating each other flesh and sucking each others bloods to stay alive. They were said to have become hunchbacked with hair covering their bodies, eating raw meat and bark from trees. In many ways today's ape (i.e., the gorilla), though, seems more sophisticated than some people today; they eat only vegetables. However, if this is true, can anyone blame Europeans for being a trifle pissed at the rest of the world, once emerging from this horrible state? Which is true, though, did man come from apes, as is rumored by the Europeans and about Oriental people, or did apes come from man, as is rumored about the Europeans?

It is seen, however, that Europeans do, in fact, invade other countries and torture and kill them for seemingly no reasons, an extremely animal-like behavior. Although, they have evolved into a very sophisticated and beautiful race of people. The people from China and India has never been recorded to have wantonly invaded and killed without reason, and whether from apes or not has given to the world two beautiful religions, as well as an extraordinary culture that enlightens and eventually might lead people to paradise on earth.

Hinduism is a glorious religion filled with amazing animation. It teaches of one hundred (100) personalities of God, and these 100 personalities can be seen in man. Moreover, as one travels, one can detect these personalities repeat themselves over and over again in all races and cultures. Have you ever met someone who reminded you so much of someone else, it was totally unbelievable? Well, you may have been witnessing two people with the same personality! Hinduism teaches of the Creator, the Sustainer, and the Destroyer. This Destroyer, Westerners refer to as Christ, the destroyer of incarnate error. People accuse Hindus as worshipping cows. Again, is it more logical to kill the cow and contract tuberculosis and other weird diseases, heart attacks included, and of course have meat for six months to a year, or let the cow live and have a work animal, beast of burden, lawn mower, milk, cheese, ice-cream, butter and so forth for fifty years? Which is more logical? The world has a lot to learn from Hindus; instead, people would rather start vicious rumors against Hindus and seek to persecute them.

Islam teaches that Cain had a twin sister named Akklia and Abel had a twin sister named Lullawa. Lullawa had a bent nose, and when Cain found out that he was meant to marry Abel's twin sister, he flipped. No matter what justifications he was given, he accepted none; he simply refused to marry Lullawa. He wanted his pretty little sister, Akklia. After killing his only brother over his beautiful twin sister, he was exiled into the East, where Easterners began. His livelihood was growing vegetables. This could well explain the people in India and their understanding of vegetarianism and their amazing beauty. However, people can believe what they want. However it may be, people should know that, just as one person can conjure up lies and vicious rumors on others, others can do the same to them. No one is free from derogatory slander or teachings of his or her race, whether it or they be true or not. The question now is whether all people can forget the past and live together? Maybe, it is better that everyone behave themselves and come to life and live forever in the flesh!

GUATAMA

Is True Love Really Such A
HORRIBLE THREAT

How many people of this generation, or even of the generation of Gautama, would leave a life of total luxury to seek solutions to problems for their lesser brothers and sisters? Most people know of none, except maybe Osama Bin Ladin. Of course, though, no one really knows Bin Ladin's motives.

Most people with money are so selfish; they don't even give to homeless or needy people. Is it not difficult to imagine millionaires cheating on taxes and complaining because poor people are given tax breaks? How horrible! Just think, people said Bill Clinton would not make a good president, because he wanted to raise taxes for rich people. Is it not the way of heaven to take from the rich and give to the poor? Besides, how did the rich become rich, except from the cheap labor of poor people? Yet, most rich people call themselves Christian, Muslim, Hindu, Jew, etc., is this not contradictory?

Howbeit, Gautama, was born near modern day Nepal, a prince. His father wanted to know, before Gautama was born, what Gautama's destiny would be; therefore, he consulted a wise sage. The wise man told Gautama's father that there were two possibilities: Gautama would either be a world conqueror, or He would resort to the life of a Buddha. His father wanting his son to be a world conqueror, asked the wise man how could Gautama's destiny be determined? The wise sage responded that if Gautama ever saw the realities of the world, he would inevitably strive to help humanity and would never be a world conqueror. Thus, before Gautama was born, his father prepared a palace for him that would keep Gautama hedged in away from the realities of the world. Even the leaves that had fallen from the trees, according to Lord,, Markman, Merrill, & White (1990), were immediately gotten rid of by apparently youthful workers on the grounds. Nothing shy of as near to perfect as possible was allowed on the grounds of the palace. Gautama was hedged in until he was an adult. Still being hedged in, Gautama became married, and he and his wife had a son.

Gautama lived this type of life until one day, when he was near twenty-nine years old; by accident, he ended up outside of his protective domain. As only fate would have it, an old man had become lost, and not knowing where he was became face to face with Gautama. They both were shocked almost out of their wits. The old man had never seen one so beautiful, and Gautama had never seen anything so horrible! Gautama did not know what the man was, but after inquiring, discovered that the man had grown old, and that everyone alive was expected to one day become old. This worried Gautama, and the next time he was wandering outside of the palace he decided to venture further. This next venture brought Gautama in the presence of a person who was sick and diseased with paleness of skin. This frightened Gautama even more than seeing the old man, and after inquiring a second time, discovered that this was a sick person, and that everyone was susceptible to sickness and disease. Gautama was so disturbed, he barely could sleep, and wanted to see more. When Gautama ventured outside of his protective domain for a third time, he saw a person who had died from an incurable affliction, and might have loss sanity at that point, had it not been for an ascetic who was present. This ascetic had an unusually wise but youthful appearance that was similar to Gautama's whose appearance had been protected from all horrors.

The ascetic saw that Gautama was impressed by his appearance and realized how much his presence relieved Gautama's anxiety. The ascetic explained the horrors of human existence to

Gautama. After this day, Gautama was never the same. Not being able to enjoy his life of wealth and happiness with his wife and son, knowing now what was going on outside of his protective domain, Gautama left all of his riches at the age of approximately twenty-nine, seeking to destroy the wickedness he had mistakenly seen.

First, Gautama wanted to discover why people became old and wanted to destroy this error. Secondly, Gautama wanted to discover what made people sick and what caused afflictions and wanted to destroy this error. Thirdly, Gautama wanted to discover what caused death and destroy this error. Finally, Gautama wanted to know how to make everyone like the ascetic whom he had been totally impressed by and who, despite the evils of the world, seemed unaffected.

Gautama, after six years of fasting, supposedly accomplished all he set out to do, but because of the prior Hinduist beliefs of his people, wanted now to discover how to die without being reborn, or without coming back. This also was said to have been accomplished. Moreover, Gautama taught others to fast. Gautama engaged in long periods of fasting for more than forty years after his enlightenment under the Bodhi Tree, where he became a Buddha.

Of course though, "Alexander the Great," somewhere around the year of 323 B.C.E., conquered many nations, with his extraordinary military campaigns. He conquered in and around various parts of India. He viciously destroyed much of what had been accomplish by Gautama the Buddha, down to the paintings and statues of Buddha, some of which were altered as well. It seems as though Alexander's ultimate mission was to destroy everything non-European and replace it with everything European. This may well account for the many parallels in the life of Buddha and the life of Jesus. They both died when they were thirty-three years of age, and they both were called the Son of God, Alexander and Jesus. How interesting?

Hinduism is a very extraordinary, and highly sophisticated religious belief; however, it seems as though people were and are controlled with fear and intimidation, especially of reincarnation. This was eventually Gautama's primary concern for himself. He did not want to return after death.

Moreover, even today, the vegetarianism practiced there is primitive, to the extent that India is believed to have the highest rate of Diabetes in the world. Beans, bread, and potatoes are starches far too potent to be digested with mere milk alone. This was also discovered by Buddha, especially upon one of his visits to China, where five-hundred Chinese Monks went out in the forests; found many rare vegetables, and prepared a dish that would feed every part of Buddha's body. How amazing! Chinese monks believed that the way a vegetable look determined what part of the body it fed (e.g., the bean because it look like the stomach, affected the stomach more than other parts of the body).

Hinduism, like Christianity and Islam, tends to become a trifle extreme (e.g., bathing in water where dead bodies are floating by, while one is bathing). Islam prohibits its believers from eating pork; therefore, Muslims tend to eat beef more extensively than others, apparently trying to make up for the pork that they do not eat. Thus, in Arabia, and other surrounding Islamic domains, where vegetarianism is not a factor, it is discovered that heart attacks are experienced more among the males in these regions than in other nations. Leather is made from cows. What is tougher than leather? How long does an individual chew on beef; before finally deciding to swallow, still realizing that the piece of beef has been altered very little? Why eat it? Hindus are accused of worshipping cows, but there philosophy is simply, "kill the cow and have discomfort and beef for several months; allow the cow to live and have milk, butter, cream, cheese, ice cream, a beast of burden, and a lawn mower for fifty years." Isn't this beautiful logic? The life span of a cow is about seventy to seventy-eight years, under pleasant conditions (more than any other land mammal).

Gautama the Buddha was very impressed with Confucius and Lao Tzu. These men were extraordinary thinkers and philosophers.

Confucianism and Taoism, especially the latter, though, express ideas concerning enlightenment from a theoretical and common sense type of learning and reasoning. Taoism, though, teaches an eventual attainment of eternal life through magical means. This is very interesting, huh? Most serious martial artists accept the logic of Confucianism and Taoism? These are two very beautiful and extremely sophisticated forms of beliefs, and Confucius and Lao Tzu were believed to be two beautiful human beings. However, would not the world itself, in fact, be this heaven that many religious people are trying to reach, if everyone would try to be more like Gautama the Buddha?

Many years ago, before other religions were allowed to be taught in America, Americans were told that people everywhere in the East worshipped Idol Gods. Have you heard of any idol gods mentioned, in this synopsis of Buddha's life? Could this have been a sinister plan to keep people ignorant of the many contributions of people of color? However, most of their colors were changed or highly altered during "Alexander's" time. Alexander the great and his men, though, are not the only conquerors who are responsible for the many variations in race and/or colors of people in the world. Hannibal and his men raped and tortured Europeans as much in thirteen years as the Moors did in seven hundred; perhaps, more viciously, though, for retaliatory reasons. Hannibal and his army spread brown hair and black eyes throughout parts of France and Spain, and resided in Italy for thirteen full years, after murdering thousands of Italians, which may explain why some Italians are so dark-skinned, and have brown eyes and black hair. Europeans do not like to hear this side of history, but are so willing to talk about slavery of people of color by Europeans. The Moors from Morocco, Africa conquered Spain and stayed there for over seven hundred years civilizing Spaniards. This may help explain why Spain was so much more civilized than other European countries, and why Spanish people of Europe have brown eyes and black hair: they look like their forefathers: Africans. Furthermore, it is documented that, while Columbus and his band of thieves were here on the North American continent handing the Native American the cross, trying to force them to believe in a White Son of God; Spanish people in Europe were worshipping the "Black Madonna." Spaniards worshipped a picture of a black woman and a male child, called the "Black Madonna," as their God for hundreds of years. Moreover, today, in parts of Spain, Italy, and France, many young people are ashamed of their parents because their parents still worship the "Black Madonna." This is similar to the shame many African American children experience in the United States, because some of their brainwashed parents still have a picture of a White man on their living room walls, calling him the only begotten son of the creator of the entire universe. Is this not ignorant? In Europe though, it is said that they have annual pilgrimages to visit and kiss the "Black Madonna," because of its healing powers. This pilgrimage is similar to Muslim's visit to the Kaaba in Mecca, Saudi Arabia. Also, in Europe, the Catholic popes are said to kiss the feet, daily, of St. Peter, who is portrayed as a black man holding the keys to heaven. Is this wild? So, you see, African Americans are not the only people of the world who are blindly seeking the truth, but still, is it not frustrating that people (black, brown, red, yellow and white) will not join in and seek salvation together?

THE FAR EAST

DOES THE FLESH NEED RELIGION TOO?

This exalted master, after entering a scheduled assembly, began to speak, and this is what he said, "having all sorts of knowledge cannot be compared to giving up seeking for anything, because this is the best of all things. Mind is not of several kinds, and there is no true doctrine which can be put into mere words. Thus, there is no more that can really be said," and he left.

A man was once seen running to the top of a hill, and once he would get to the very top, he would yell as loudly as he could to produce an echo in the valley below. Then, he would race back to the valley to find the echo. However, of course, once he reached the valley, the echo would have gone. Then, he would repeat the sequence. This has been compared to leaving the near to seek the far. Once an individual has arrived to that which was considered far, it becomes near, and what was considered near, initially, has now become far. An individual could spend eons upon eons living this type of life. The near will always be near, and the far will always be far, regardless of what. Thus, an individual can know everything that takes place under the sky, without making a single journey.

An individual should learn to not think in terms of good and evil. Once, an individual learns not to think in terms of good, and not to think in terms of evil, one need only then return to what that individual was before his or her mother or father was born. These previously mentioned proverbs are taken from Confucian and Taoist doctrines.

It seems every country has similar doctrines to each other. In other words, all human beings hold the same to be sacred. The golden rule, to be more specific, is in every single established religion. "Do unto others and theirs as you would have others do unto you and yours, and never do that which you would not have known."

The trinity, in some form or the other, can also be found in most established religions. Does that mean that there is a man somewhere up above the clouds or up in the air sitting on some sort of exalted seat or throne, or that some man or woman is beneath the earth's crust dwelling in a fiery furnace or environment? Of course not!

Can God or this supposed creator of all things exist in an image similar to man and not be human? Of course!

The question now becomes, if an individual who believed in God or this supposed creator of all things were here on this gracious earth two thousand years longer than another different individual who also believed in God or a supposed creator who created all things, who would most likely know more about this creator of all things? The eastern civilized world has existed hundreds of years longer than the western civilized world! The Martial Arts were founded by the eastern world. Now, the questions become, what is the Martial Arts and what good is the Martial Arts to man, other than a tool to kick or chop someone into oblivion?

Man has attempted for years to understand the sayings of wise sages and prophets, to no avail. Man, as a whole, is still where he was before those prophets came and now since they are gone. Moreover, many methods have been devised to aid Westerners in understanding wise or prophetic sayings, and Westerners have been helped a little but not to any serious mathematical extent. Is it the Westerner or is it the method that the Westerner is using? It is obvious that it could very easily be deduced to being the latter! Going to church on Sunday and getting pushed down under water have certainly proven to be failing methods. God does not dwell in temples made by human hands (Acts 7:48).

Jesus, of the Christian's Holy Bible, says, "if you have faith as that of a mustard seed, you shall say to this mountain, Move from here to there, and it shall move; and nothing shall be impossible to you. "But this kind of faith does not go out except by prayer and fasting" (Matthew 17:20-21)

In John 5:24, Jesus says, "Truly, truly, I say to you, he who hears my word and believes him who sent me, hath everlasting life and shall not come into condemnation, but has passed from death unto life." In John 8:51, Jesus says, "Verily, Verily, I say unto you, if a man keeps my saying, he shall never taste death." All of you who do not believe can read the following five or six verses and will see that they are actually talking about physical death, as they are in the entire chapter of Ezekiel Eighteen (18).

In John 11:25-26, Jesus says, "he that believe in me, though he were dead, yet shall he live" (speaking of the resurrection), but continues by saying, "and whosoever live and believe in me shall never die," and asked Martha if she believed in that (making a clear distinction between the two beliefs). Open your eyes people?

People boast of having been baptized or born again, and they use profanity like a heathen who has no religion at all; they commit adultery; they steal and lie; and they do many other things that even they themselves admit is wrong and against the very God they serve. Have they really been baptized? Most of them have! Have they been born again or born of God? Of course not! Yes, they have been dunked under water and made wet, and if the water was clean and they were dirty, surely they returned from the water cleaner on the outside, but is this baptism. It is certainly not the baptism of the Christ of the Christian's Holy Bible!

Whosoever is born of God does not commit sin, and he cannot sin, because he is born of God (1 John 3:9). Thus, whoever claims that he or she has been born again, but they say they still sin, they are liars! They do not know what they are talking about. They obviously believe in that which is symbolic and not real.

Many people do not have the faith to believe that God lives inside of them, and are forced by this belief to believe only in a God who lives high up in the sky away from them, where he obviously belongs, when it comes to some people (smile). But what about what is written?

Do you not know that you are the temple of God, and that the spirit of God lives in you? If any man defile the temple of God, him shall God destroy; for the temple of God is holy, which temple you are" (1 Corinthians 3:16). Stop deceiving yourself! This is clear!

People a long time ago used to retreat to a cave or a deserted area to ponder or meditate upon prophetic sayings, attempting to understand them more clearly, and still they could not understand them. It is very difficult too for an individual to discipline oneself! Thus, the Martial Arts was discovered or developed to help the sinner or the one who could not believe on his or her own. The Martial Arts shows one moving from an inferior being to a more superior one, stage after stage after stage. One then begins to understand that there is no limit to what the mind can accomplish. Finally, a practitioner learns to believe in the Tao (a being that lives within).

Is it not horrible that some people have to eat a whole cow to know that they are eating beef? Are you one of those people? Can you believe upon hearing the thunder roar and the lighting strike and seeing the sun rise each and everyday or your life, or do you, as well, need the Martial Arts?

Although very few people know about or are familiar with the Boxer Rebellion, there is probably next to no one who does not know about or are not familiar with "Bruce Lee."

The Boxer Rebellion, in essence is a war involving China that stemmed from foreigners sending drugs (Heroin) and religious doctrine into China. Both the drugs and the religious doctrine, to Chinese, corrupted China or brought corruption to the Chinese people. Thus, China sought to rid the country of both the drugs and Christianity, both of which were seen by Chinese to be meant to bring death to Chinese people. China in all cases burned any illegal drugs discovered, and in some cases killed foreign religious teachers. China invented gun powder as well as superior physical fighting skills; however, both were dangerous as well as beneficial to its people. Therefore, both were outlawed: guns and kung fu. Nevertheless, after the heroin was burned and ministers killed, war emerged, and many Chinese were killed by foreigners (Europeans), despite Masters attempting to teach Chinese that nothing dead could harm them (bullets) and that they had nothing to fear. Chinese could not comprehend the master's teaching and many fell by the foreign guns.

Finally, China having the fear of losing too many Chinese to foreign guns consented to a treaty. The treaty involved China giving up Hong Kong and many valuable ports to pay for economical damages claimed to have been suffered by Europeans.

After the end of the war, China developed an unwritten law that no non-Chinese, mainly Europeans, could ever be shown true kung-fu! Bruce Lee felt that because he was Chinese, his birth right entitled him to true kung-fu. Bruce Lee was said to have been sneaking illegally in and out of China stealing kung-fu and paying other Chinese to steal kung-fu for him as well. It is further rumored that Bruce Lee was detected on some occasions and warned to bring it to a halt, learn his history and cease trying to learn kung-fu secrets to teach Europeans. Of course, Bruce continued to get better and better at an abnormally rapid rate and continued to teach Europeans whatever he learned. The author has personally witnessed actual photos taken by photographers in Hollywood California showing Bruce Lee leaping at heights higher than humanly possible, without the aid of trampolines, before his death in 1973. The rest is history!

What makes the Martial Arts so unique is that it includes the discipline man needs to conceive the spirit. The Western world has the skill needed but not the discipline! Thus, Westerners are restricted to physical feats and not those requiring full use of the mind (i.e., defying gravity, by walking on thin elevated rice paper, elevation or mental telepathy, and the seeming impossible feats of speed and strength shown by the Oriental Martial Arts Masters.

Come To Life, people and leave the animal flesh alone. Vegetarianism is the true path to understanding God, Allah, Jehovah or whatever or whoever you call the Supreme Being!

DEATH AS WE KNOW IT

CAN PHYSICAL DEATH
BE AVOIDED?

Where do people go when or after they die? Well, the answer is simple. The body goes to hell and the spirit goes to heaven! Although this is true, do not let this frighten you? Hell is the grave, and heaven is where the birds fly and where the planets and other celestial bodies preside. Imagine a long line of machines lining the ocean shores and each time a machine is built, it is place somewhere within the ranks of this line. Imagine each machine being built to last forever, with proper maintenance and care. Now, imagine that if each machine does not receive proper care and maintenance, each machine will operate unpredictably for approximately seventy years, give or take a few years. Imagine each machine requiring a full gallon of ocean water to operate sufficiently, and this gallon of water, of course, comes from the ocean. Imagine, each machine that receives proper maintenance and care is constantly visited by the maker, being cared for and maintained (i.e., shelter from disasters and parts repaired and corrected when necessary). Now, imagine the other machines not receiving proper care and maintenance (i.e., not receiving shelter from disasters and not having parts repaired and corrected when necessary). Now, imagine all of the possible things that can happen to these machines that do not receive this care from the maker of the machine. Some of the machines that become damaged by disasters will break and the gallon of water will run back into the ocean from whence it came. Some of the machines that are allowed to grow old without maintenance and care will have its gallon of water extracted from it by the maker and cast back into the ocean from whence it came. Imagine the machines being the body made from the earth. Imagine the ocean being heaven and the gallon of water being that spirit in all living beings that has been given to them by heaven. The body goes back to the earth from whence it came, and the spirit goes back into the atmosphere of heaven from whence it came. The marvelous thing, though, is that just like the ocean and the earth, heaven is ALIVE, believe it! Oh! Yes, that's right, life, everlasting life...does a person have to die? Is there no possible way of avoiding the physical death? First of all, do you believe in a God who would viciously tease you by giving you something so precious as "life" and then snatching it back whenever that God pleases, regardless of whether you have been a saint or sinner? Do you really believe in a God like this, or will you admit that the deaths that people die are determined by those people and the way in which they live? Aren't you sick and tired of death, or are you one of the people who would rather try to get rid of the "law" (which you cannot get rid of), than to get rid of death (which you can get rid of)?

Were Adam and Eve going to live forever if they had not sinned? Are people beyond correction or repair? With God, are all things possible? Is the sting of death, really, sin? Is it possible not to sin? Why would people be cautioned, by God, not to sin, if it is impossible not to sin? So then, are people faithless, continually consuming anything they want to eat, drink, inject, smoke, inhale, ingest, snort, drop, lick, suck, sniff, chew, or dip, and dying all sorts of mysterious, weird, and sometimes vicious deaths, or is God foolish for asking people to live righteously, knowing they cannot? Thus, the question finally emerges, can people live forever? The answer is yes, and if you think about it, you will agree! Anyone can live as long as he or she wants to live. How? By using common sense, and by applying that common sense to one's daily endeavors!

The religion of the elders was that anything that caused unhappiness, grief, pain, sorrow, or sadness, or anything that caused death, sickness, and discomfort was considered as evil or bad, and anything that caused joy, happiness, good health, and comfort was considered as good. Remember, the patriarchs (e.g., Adam, Noah, Methuselah) live almost a thousand years. There were no personifications of God, a superior man who live beyond the clouds, and the Devil, a man who lived under the ground, as people understand and recognize them today in religions like Christianity and Islam. Acts that lead to misfortune, death, or illness were not allowed and considered, by society, as acts of infidelity and/or evil. Only lifestyles that lead to health, wealth, fortune, and beauty were encouraged, and everything in the universe was considered as purposeful; although, everything was not considered as food. Again, everything was considered as good, but everything was not considered as good to put into one's mouth as food for proper rejuvenation. For every action, there is an equal but opposite reaction, right? Cause and effect; nothing can neither be created nor destroyed; do you remember all that junk? Does the reader agree with these laws or not?

If you, the reader, were driving an automobile down the street, and all of a sudden the automobile shut off, for no apparent reason, and it was allowed to coast to the side of the street. Many of your friends stopped and tried to give their advice and their assistance, but no one could get it started. Finally, one person stopped, and after carefully looking over the automobile's engine said, "I don't know why this automobile won't start, there is nothing whatsoever wrong with it!" Would you believe that? Of course not! This person might not know what is wrong with this automobile, but if this automobile is supposed to start, and it will not start; there is most definitely something wrong with it! If all the components are there, and if all the components are operable, then, and only then, it should by all means start. Therefore, one is to conclude that either all the components are not present, or one or more of its' vital parts will not work (are inoperable). Does the reader agree? Because everyone's set of values might be slightly different, one must use a trifle bit of common sense, when parting the truth from the lie. Nevertheless, if the reader agrees that, even an automobile, an object made by man, must have something wrong with it, to just quit or cut off; then, the reader should also agree that the human body, the ultimate creation by God, the Creator, must also have something wrong with it to die or to stop.

If one would go to any cemetery and dig up any body, from any grave, one could determine, by performing a professional autopsy, what contributed to that individual's death. Whatever part of that individual's body that was defective or damaged will show up during the autopsy. For example, if an individual smoked excessively, there lungs might appear defective, faulty, or damaged; if one drank alcohol excessively, other vital internal organs might appear defective, faulty, or damaged; if one had been a liar, a cheat, a thief, a whore, a whore monger, a murderer, an adulterer, an inconsiderate or disrespectful person, a two-faced or back-stabbing person, a careless or reckless person, or if one had been any other kind of person who was living a lifestyle that was totally contrary to what God has ordained in every established religion; then, the autopsy might reveal evidences of viruses or fatal diseases, stab wounds, bullet wounds, cuts and bruises, parts missing, burns, evidence of torture, swelling or swollen parts, poison, evidence of suffocation, and the list goes on; and finally, if one had lived what is referred to as a "good" carnal life: eating mostly the permitted foods, usually excessively; drinking in moderation, usually; partaking of all the carnal aspects of life in moderation, usually; treating everyone as one wished to be treated, mostly; but, nevertheless, this person did not fast the small sins from the body, as was necessary, and those sins (in the forms of lawful and unlawful meats (animal blood), grain, chemicals, spices, and drink) were allowed to, grow, build and become compressed, until one had literally become that which he or she has consumed; one might then have suffered a variety of fatal illnesses, and an autopsy might reveal merely an old horribly ugly wrinkled face and body, with the head and body filled with almost all defective parts (referred to as old age). The proper foods must be eaten, and fasting is imperative.

A disbeliever's first defense against any implication that some foods are bad for human consumption is that his or her grandmother ate pork, catfish, crayfish, raccoons, and rabbit, and she lived to be eighty-five years old. However, they do not mention that their poor grandmother had become so ugly most people could not stand to look at her, that she looked like she was eight hundred and fifty instead of eighty-five. She also, most likely, had been in pain for the last ten to fifteen years of her life, and maybe more, suffering from high blood pressure, rheumatism, arthritis, heart problems, gastric disturbances, constipation, loss of bladder control, headaches, loss of sight, loss of hearing, and swollen gums resulting from her badly needed false teeth resulting from all the sugar she ate, constant indigestion, and many other complications. Their grandmother looked so badly before she died, she was almost unbearable to look upon, and they brag that she lived eighty-five years. This is horrible! They should be enraged that their grandmother had been deceived into thinking that someone else (Jesus) had already suffered, 2,000 years ago, for something that another (their grandmother) did to her self, just recently!

Exercise programs have sprung up throughout the world, and people are exercising frantically trying to look younger. Strenuous exercise makes the body appear younger; although, the fanatics are usually in pain, but what about their faces, the age is apparent; and in the female population of body builders, the faces are sometimes horrible. People meet every day and exercise until they break out into a drenching sweat. A new car, driven slowly and driven short distances, last much longer than a car that is driven very fast and driven very long distances. Imagine the mileage gauge on the speedometer, in a car, what does the mileage tell the driver. That is right; it tells the driver when the car is going to be ready to start having mechanical problems. What about when it goes past 100,000 miles? Please see the similarity? Over-exercising is not wise; exercise is good, but over-exercising causes an individual to age much faster than an individual who does not over-exercise, providing they both eat animal flesh.

Imagine an individual who is of average weight for his or her height, and to sustain this, the individual would have to eat one to three not-too-small/not-too-large meals combined of all kinds of meats and all kinds of vegetables, daily, and get five to eight hours of sleep most nights (maybe drinking and/or smoking moderately and possibly having experimented with drugs or marijuana). Now, add to this by saying that this person, doing this would be expected to live until he or she was about seventy to one-hundred years old, probably having lost all of his or her teeth; experienced many kinds of physical ailments, and may have had some sort of surgery.

Now, imagine two other individuals. The first individual, being an extremist in the negative sense, ate three huge meals combined of all kinds of meats and all kinds of vegetables, and he or she also ate between meal snacks, daily; he or she drank and/or smoke heavily and used drugs and marijuana whenever possible; and he or she got very little sleep. What outcome in this situation would be expected?

The second individual, however, was an extremist in the positive sense, ate one meal per day consisting of vegetables, grains, honey, and milk products and sometimes fasted; drank mild liquors and smoked marijuana on special occasions only, and got eight hours of sleep each night. Is it not obvious that if one compared these three individuals, the results would probably be that the negative extremist would not live as long as the individual in the middle, and the positive extremist would probably live much longer? Now, if one added other negative behaviors to the negative extremist, or compounded the current ones, the negative extremist would be expected to die even sooner. Would you not agree? Then, on the other hand, if one subtracted some of the negative behaviors from the positive extremist, say take away some or all of the alcohol, drugs, and/or marijuana, the positive extremist would be expected to live even longer. Would you not agree to this as well?

The Holy Spirit or that essence that lives inside of all living things should be looked upon as an assessor who settles at the beginning of each day. Once an individual becomes a vegetarian, if an individual fasted one day and abstained from substance, the spirit, when it returns to awaken the body after a night's sleep will not take away a day of life from the individual; if an individual has fasted two days and has abstained from substance, the spirit, when it returns to awaken the body after a second night's sleep awards the body an additional day of life to the individual's youth (subtracting a day from one's age). On the other hand, if an individual has eaten in excess or has provided the body with a day's sustenance of food, the spirit, when it returns to awaken the body, requires from or subtracts from that body a day of life or that equal to the excess (adding a day to one's age). Every time the spirit and the body comes in contact (after every deep sleep), the body undergoes a physical change, be it aging or revitalization. This is the power of the essence of all life, and the ever-constant law of the yin and the yang. The adding to and subtracting from the individual is done so gradually, it will go unnoticed for years; therefore, anyone who decides to begin fasting should not be disappointed after fasting one day and seeing no results. Imagine traveling and going five miles past a desired highway. Is it feasible to expect to come back three miles and be able to start where one left off? Certainly not! One would have to travel the entire five miles back. Likewise, eventually, one, whether ninety years old or thirty-nine, will have to rid the body of all the sin he or she has put into the body. However, because the body is believed to renew itself every seven to ten years, if one abstained from meat, received the proper nourishment, and fasted rigorously, one could be right at the threshold of becoming anew in a span of seven to ten years.

On the following page are a list of a composition of diets and a list of foods one might choose. This diet is very similar to the hospital diets.

IS LOGICAL THINKING

... REQUIRED IN OVEREATING?

It is believed that man is of the garden and, therefore, must eat from the garden; and the beast, because it is of the field was meant to eat of the field. The more delicate vegetation (garden vegetables) requires less water than the less delicate vegetable. Black-eyed peas, pinto beans, white beans, butter beans, navy beans, dried corn or corn bread, etc., all seem to be too harsh for the human body.

Staying away from these harsh starches, as much as possible, could cause one to be very comfortable. However, upon first becoming a vegetarian, these field vegetables will give one strength and enable one to use up the filth that is causing age; nevertheless, after the filth is gone, these field vegetables in their natural form will cause harm, being too potent will cause one's face to appear swollen, diabetes, glaucoma, arthritis, severe constipation and stomach cramps, and more, but above all, that unsightly obese appearance.

Calories = 2,100 From Vegetables, Fruit & Milk Products

Protein = 95 gm From Vegetables, Fruit & Milk Products

Fat = 91 gm From Vegetables, Fruit & Milk Products

Carbohydrates = 196 gm. From Vegetables, Fruit & Milk Products

Fruits:

Good fruits to eat are apples, apricots, bananas, berries, grapefruit, melons, oranges, peaches, pears, pineapples, tangerines.

Vegetables:

Good vegetables are asparagus, avocado, beets, broccoli, brussels sprouts, cabbage, cauliflower, carrots, celery, corn, turnips, cucumbers, egg plants, lima beans, onions, peas, radishes, sauerkraut, squash, string beans, and tomatoes (milk, lettuce, mushrooms, and nuts can be used as frequently as one wishes; however, a little milk and very few nuts will suffice, or constipation and/or cramping will result; the more delicate the milk and the nuts, the better).

Proteins:

Loma Linda, near San Bernardino, California, and Worthington, in Ohio, produce health foods from rice, beans, and wheat, sometimes in the form of gluten and tofu. These proteins are very healthy and very tasty and come in many forms.

Sometimes the body has to be conditioned before it realizes that vegetables can be made to look like the dishes mankind has used the animal to create. Hamburgers, hot dogs, meat loaf, bologna, salami, and any other dish, with the exception of the construction of skeletons or bones, which to most people are unnecessary; e.g., neck-bones, t-bone steaks, drumsticks, pork-chops, etc. can be constructed from vegetables. Most people are sophisticated enough to enjoy filleted and sliced meats; these are very easy to imitate.

Complications:

If one is experiencing diabetes or multiple sclerosis, one should learn to sometimes avoid, if not avoid altogether, especially in large and continuous quantities sugar, honey, candy, cake, pie, pastries, custards, puddings, ice creams, caffeine (coffee and strong tea), carbonated sodas, potatoes, rice, grapes, plums, figs, dates, cherries, raisins, spaghetti, macaroni, noodles, wines, sweetened cocktails, cordials, beer (field peas, beans, and other grains that have to be boiled excessively before eating are too strong for the human body).

Club sodas, weak teas, no-cal beverages (except cola) dry ginger ale, whiskeys and other distilled liquors all can be used moderately; although, liquor will cramp, can cause impotency, and will cause headaches after excessive usage, be that usage small or large. You must be especially careful when drinking carbonated beverages. They are bad for the heart!

Illicit Drugs:

Beer can bloat the stomach, and marijuana causes overeating; if overeating could be avoided, moderate use might never injure, and might even help. Hard drugs can cause one to eat animal and possibly human flesh. Hard liquor hardens arteries and vital organs.

COULD HUMANITY HAVE TRAVELED THIS FAR...

...WITHOUT THINKING LOGICALLY?

Reader, if a human body starts out as an infant of twenty inches long, and if the only thing this individual does is put certain things in its mouth, and it gets bigger and bigger, is it not obvious that whatever this individual is putting in his or her mouth is making this individual bigger? Thus, is it obvious that a person is exactly what he or she eats and can logically be nothing else? Therefore, just for the sake of argument, if there is a God, and there are clean and unclean or permitted and forbidden plants and animals, would it not be logical to assume that if one ate the unclean or forbidden plants and animals, or if one defile the body in some other manner, one would probably die!

If this is too extreme, at least admit that a person would die much sooner and more painfully than a person who attempted to eat according to God's written word or according to his or her own common sense?

Imagine one living in the midst of a garden filled with many different kinds of precious fruit, vegetables, and mild nuts, and then of course, imagine many different kinds of birds and animals as well. What logical individual, without ever killing or ever seeing any animal or bird stalked, terrorized, killed and eaten, would know to kill an animal or bird and devour it? Imagine stripping it out of its hide, bursting it down to its intestines, while blood is squirting and flowing everywhere. What rational being would choose this type of violent behavior, instead of eating the many beautiful kinds of fruit, vegetables, and mild nuts which seem to be there for every living thing? None! In fact, cannibalism and/or meat-eating seem to be a result of persons being exiled away from all the abundance of God's precious vegetation.

Filth breeds filth. All of the animals seen today were not here originally, and all of the animals that were here originally are not all here today. In fact, mankind is responsible for many different breeds of animals, birds, fish, reptiles, and plants existing today.

Many people will say this is preposterous or this is crazy, and that God is responsible for all the animals and plants in existence. Well, it seems discussion is in order. Many hunters will agree that they have traveled and hunted throughout many strange woods and have never seen a herd of Doberman, a herd of cocker spaniel, or a herd of poodles or Siamese cats. A nectarine is a cross between a peach and an apricot, a mule is not an original animal, and the list goes on. All the different kinds of chickens, swine, cattle, birds, cats, dogs, horses, etc., etc., etc., are the doings of man. Many plants and trees are results of experiments of mankind. Please understand this? It is two-thousand years after the time of Jesus, and people still expect to see the Christ, if they see him, riding on a donkey with twelve other men walking beside him wearing sandals with ragged cloths wrapped around them for clothing. The mention of Christ in modern times doing modern things modern ways, with modern machinery or technology seems to bewilder people. How dumbfounded or dormant can a mind allow itself to become?

Wake up people, do you really believe in a God who would create you to be in agony, to suffer, to be at the mercy of evil people, and to die a horrible death, regardless of whether you did everything bad or everything good, and there is no way around it? What kind of God is this? This is not God's way; this is the Devil's way! Read the Bible for yourselves, it tells you all the way through it that one can live forever. In fact, the Bible's total implication and/or insinuation are that with God all things are possible. Do you believe in God, or do you believe that you are condemned to experience the same misfortunes as others who have obviously transgressed many of God's commandments, even though you are not transgressing any commandments? Does this make sense to you? Do you treat the people who treat you good the same as you treat the people who treat you badly? Do you love them the same? Do you invite them all into your household to spend the night with you? Do you buy them Christmas presents? Please do not lie? God knows your heart! You hate evil the same as the author does! Why should God treat evil people the same as he treats people who are trying to do right? Why should Christ cast all the good people into the lake of fire to burn for however long, and then place all the bad people in "New Jerusalem" to live in comfort forever? Is this common sense?

As soon as good people develop the courage and the common sense to hate evil and love good and to destroy evil and to promote good, the world, as we know it, will become the heaven people pray for God to build for them. Everything that one can imagine in any heaven is right here on earth without the presence of evil. Think about it.

Most people ask the questions, "then why have people been dying all these years, if people can live as long as they want to," "why hasn't anyone else said that people can live as long as they want," "why haven't I heard anything like this before, except from you," or "so you're trying to say that just because you eat nothing but vegetables, you're supposed to live forever, huh?"

These are all valid questions, but are usually questions from people who have not given it any thought and do not plan to give it any thought because they delight in evil and sin; from people who are afraid to give it thought because of the many vices they might have to give up; from people who will not allow themselves to give it any thought because they have been brainwashed into thinking there is only one way, and no one can tell them anything they don't already know; and from people who allow others to live their lives for them.

Nevertheless, these questions deserve answers; however, these answers, also, deserve some consideration and require that they be given some serious thought; but then, what is more serious than death?

First of all, people have been dying all these hundreds of years, because of their ignorance, their stubbornness, their laziness, their negligence, their lack of trust, their lack of willpower, their infidelity, and surely, if the reader thinks about it, the reader can come up with many other reasons people have been dying.

Secondly, no one else has probably said this to you, because, either they have not studied in this area enough to have this understanding, or they are in high places and understand what is being said, but they feel that you are beyond being taught to be righteous, or they feel that if everyone were equal, the rich would not be rich and beyond working to earn a living, would then have to work like everyone else, and they are purposely keeping the truth from you.

Thirdly, in response to the question why no one has heard anything like this before, except from the author; well, the point is, every religion and/or holy book is saying just this; especially the Holy Bible. If one reads the book of Ezekiel, chapter eighteen, one will see that the entire chapter explains why a person is allowed to die and why if a person lived a certain way that person could not die. Matthew 5: 48 tells people to be perfect, but people say no one can be perfect. If this is true, why would Jesus tell one to be perfect, knowing one could not be perfect? Is someone not being foolish? The Wisdom of Solomon in the Catholic bible says that man through his disobedience and ignorance summoned death! John 8:51 says if a person believes in Jesus words they would never see death. In John fourteen, Jesus says that anyone can be just like him, even better, Jesus says out of his own mouth. So, why are people reluctant to live like Jesus?

Why do people say they follow Jesus, admit that Jesus probably was Jewish, and admit that

Jesus probably did not eat pork or any other unclean beast, foul, fish, or plant, but feel they can do whatever they wish and still be following Jesus. Is this not madness? If Jesus is traveling eastward, and another being is traveling southward, is that other being following Jesus?

Is the world going crazy? People feel that they will have no physical body in "heaven;" however, it is obvious, they are talking about New Jerusalem, since heaven is where the moon is, the sun and the stars are, and where the birds of the air fly; and since hell and the lake of fire are not the same thing (Revelation 20:14). Nevertheless, in Revelations 22:2-5, it plainly says that there will be fruit to eat and that the leaves from the tree of life are for healing the people. In John eleven, Jesus plainly tells Martha that people have two ways to go: (1) they can believe in the resurrection, or (2) they can believe in Jesus as they live to the extent that they would never see death. Remember, Jesus taught his followers to be born again, to be baptized of the water and the spirit, and to be prepared to receive the Holy Ghost.

Finally, the eating of clean foods is only the beginning of enlightenment and the cleansing of the body and soul; one must also train the mind and heart to practice pure thoughts and pure feelings. Moreover, one must follow the Ten Commandments and as many more commandments as possible that teach one to be good and kind to oneself and to one's fellow. One must not only be a vegetarian, eating all the clean foods, but one must also believe in oneself and one's creator, especially the god within. This is a must! The more powerful one's creator, the more powerful is oneself!

One should never let anyone else interpret the scriptures for them; instead, one should read the scriptures, as they are, for oneself, and believe in them as they are written. If anyone tries to interpret the scriptures, to one, by saying, "what that means is..." Simply refer that person to Revelations 22:18, where it says that "anyone who takes from the words of this book shall have his or her name taken out of the lamb's book of life, and if anyone adds to the words of this book, the plagues in this book will be added unto them," and tell them that the words mean what they say, and they say what they mean, or they would most assuredly say something else! Does this make sense? People think that everything in the bible is symbolic. This is ridiculous; however, some things are symbolic. What is really symbolic, most people take literally. For example, the idea that one person can die for another, this is most definitely symbolic. Many people believe that Jesus died for them. It seems this means that Jesus proved that one could live in a sinful world and yet be sinless, and by this could not die. Remember Bruce Lee's "Chinese Connection," "How can a healthy man die?" For the ones of "you who have to eat a whole cow to know that you are eating beef," I have given you everything you need. Stop being ironic and leave the sinful death-summoning foods, drinks, and behaviors alone?

Examine the picture on the back cover of this book and explain to yourself what it means. Imagine people not committing those things. Would they be out there? Of course they would not! How?

Why misinterpret the Bible and say that everything God made is good, pretending that you really think that this means that God made everything for food? Stop continuing to die in your silly belief and irony? Learn to adjust to vegetarianism and humanitarianism, follow the golden rule, fast, and live forever if you wish. Now that you know that your destiny is in your own hands, "come to life and liver forever in the flesh!"

EIGHT SERIOUS STEPS TO

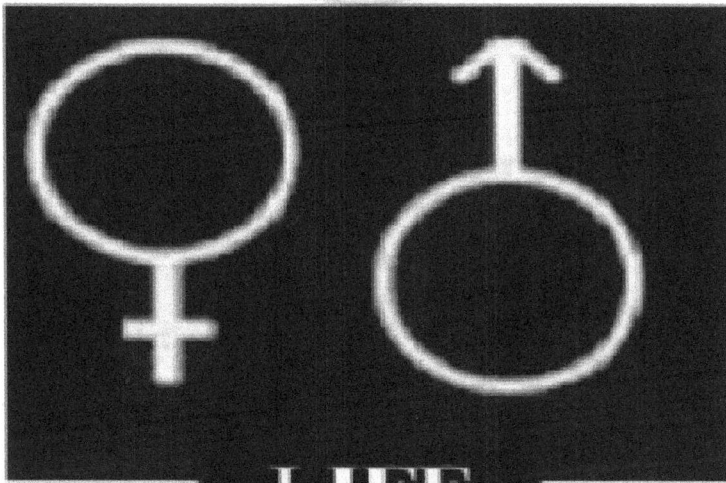

LIFE

PHYSICALLY LIVING FOREVER

T he world is set up to function as it was meant to function. Nothing can or will stop that! Therefore, the individual must adjust to the world; the world does not have to adjust to the individual.

Every tub was meant to sit on its own bottom! Moreover, you cannot live other peoples' lives for them; you can only suggest to them what you think is right. It is up to them, if they wish, to adjust accordingly!

There are many consistent sets of personality traits that differentiate "believers" from "non-believers" across a variety of situations. However, there is nothing that states that it is totally inevitable for an individual to change one way or the other or to act as they currently act. Many individuals have traveled in one direction much further than others, and other individuals have traveled in the opposite directions much further than others. No two individuals, even "identical twins," are completely the same, and having different experiences when separated from each other, from time to time, makes them even more unalike. Even two cloned individuals would end up with scars that would make them distinguishable. Therefore, I think it is safe to say that no two individuals are completely alike! Nevertheless, there are steps that individuals (humans) can use to attain immortality on earth. Some of these steps, however, might be wider, taller, and/or longer for some than for others. It depends on the length of the steps they take or have already taken; the length of their legs; and the distances from the depths or heights from which they might have to travel. These steps are as follows:

Step One

There must be a realization that there is a light that shines inside of every living thing! That light belongs entirely to the individual in whom it resides! That light is the life of the individual in whom it resides and without this light there can be no life!

Step Two

There must be a realization that the light that shines inside of every living thing is protected by the owner's compatibility with the universe! That means that the individual in whom the light shines must realize that he or she must strive to be one with the universe by living in a manner that will not intentionally destroy any aspect of the universe!

Step Three

There must be a realization that the light that shines inside of every living thing varies from one group or class of life to the other! That means that the light that shines inside of a skunk, although from the same source, is not the same quantity or specificity of light as that of the whale or whooping crane, etc. This means that the light of the living thing in which it resides determines the individual's features. The features determine the purpose. For the sake of the ironic individual, this does not mean that because an individual looks like a hog or an anteater that he or she will inevitably go out from day to day and wallow around in mud or search through the woods eating ants, but rather it suggests that the diet of either him or her or his or her parents was distorted or irregular to this extent! Know that you will inevitably become what you eat! Know also that what you eat determines whether you remain compatible with the light that resides in you

Step Four

There must be a realization that your diet must depict that you are not intentionally trying to destroy any aspect of the universe! You must eat only foods that replenish themselves! You must not eat anything that has ever been alive! You must also wean yourself from eating any aspect of anything that has ever been alive (i.e., eggs, milk, cheese, butter, lard, etc.)!

Step Five

You must practice with diet until there is an understanding of which foods give adequate supplies of proteins, carbohydrates, minerals, vitamins, fats, and water! You must practice until you know how to balance your proteins, minerals, carbohydrates, vitamins, fats, and water! These proteins, carbohydrates, minerals, vitamins, fats, and water must come from foods that replenish themselves! If any vegetable, fruit, nut, grain, root, or any other plant causes bloating, gas, diarrhea, constipation, cramps, or any other discomfort, discontinue eating them and learn to eat the ones that you like and that agrees with your digestive system. Learning to eat properly is done by trial and error. It takes about seven years to completely change your body into a clean vegetarian's body where it is compatible with the light that shines within it.

Step Six

There must be a realization that your daily actions must depict that you are not intentionally trying to destroy any aspect of the universe! You must treat every living being as you want to be treated! Again, for the sake of the ironic individual, this does not mean that you should go out and begin making love to all the insects and animals. It means that you should not intentionally harm any living being that is not trying to harm you! It also means that you should learn to avoid other living things that would intentionally harm you!

Step Seven

There must be a realization that even though your diet is good, you must learn to rid the body of an excess of stored food. This means that you should be lean and shapely; this way, the light can do its job and keep you healthy. Stored food on the body will wrinkle and decay and sometimes even before then can cause extreme discomfort! Learn to look in the mirror (nude) and tell your self whether you have consumed too much or too little of (any) of the six basic nutrients (i.e., proteins, carbohydrates, mineral, vitamins, fats, or water). Most people who have the nerve to get (nude) in front of the mirror will see that they are eating too many carbohydrates and consuming too much fat. All an individual has to do to correct this irregularity in form (i.e., ugly body) is to abstain from so much fat (i.e., greasy foods) and so many carbohydrates (i.e., rice, beans, breads, noodles, macaroni, spaghetti, potatoes, etc.) and he or she will become shapely and beautiful. Once vegetarianism has been accomplished, a perfect weight is one pound for every one-half inch of height! This way, beauty can be maintained and the light can provide its protection. This means that a five-foot human being should never weigh very much more than (5FTX24LB) one hundred and twenty pounds of vegetarian weight.

Step Eight

Stay on the path and keep the mind ever on the light that shines within you and in all other living beings. Help preserve the universe. How can you die?

Cause & Effect Reasoning

If you were to perform an autopsy on any living thing that died, especially humans, you would discover the cause of death. For example, if a person died of excessive smoking, you would probably find something wrong with his or her heart, lungs, throat, etc. If a person died of excessive drinking of alcohol, you would probably find something wrong with his or her heart, stomach, liver, throat, etc. If a person died of lying, stealing, cheating, or meddling, you would probably find a bullet, stick, brick, skillet, or knife wound or some other wound to his or her heart, throat, head, chest, stomach, back, etc.

If a person died of meat-eating or not fasting, you would probably find something wrong with many parts of his or her body or simply find an old ugly, horribly wrinkled, distorted, worn-out, nasty-looking, smelly, and unsightly corpse that has developed after years and years of horrible pain an agony due to down right irony, stubbornness, and closed-mindedness. Come to life people, and live forever in the flesh!

For the Christian reader, in your bible, there are many scriptures that validate and support the idea of immortality or living forever in the flesh. For your enjoyment, if it does not offend you nor violate your belief, read these few verses. It is not necessary for life every lasting, it is just a simple confirmation, if you are Christian or if you simply love reading.

"You shall know the truth, and the truth shall make you free!" Please examine the following scriptures: John 8: 34; John 9: 31; Ecclesiastes 9:5; Ezekiel 18: 20-32; John 5: 24; John 8: 51-55; and John 11: 26.

In the beginning of the book, the concept of the Grim Reaper was referenced as someone who the world must unite and bury. Actually the Grim Reaper is merely a concept of death, a concept society in its fears created. The so-called Angel of Death and the Angel of Life are one and the same. As usual, though, man blames something else other than himself for his self-appointed fate.

If there was an individual who was alive and had fasted as a vegetarian to the extent that he or she would appear as a skeleton who wore a robe. He or she would be closer to the light than anyone else (i.e., all others) and could only be a good person! Rid yourself of your evil flesh and stop blaming others, especially an entity referred to as "God" for (your) death!

Bibliography

Ali, M. M. (1973). The Holy Qur'an. Arabic Text, English Translation and Commentary (sixth ed.) Lahore, Pakistan: Ahmadiyya Anjuman Isha'at Islam, Incorporated.

Aquina, T. (140 A.D.). The gospel according to Thomas. Coptic text established and translated by A. Guillaumont, H.-Ch. Puech, G. Quispel, W. Till and Yassah 'Abd Al Masih (Leiden E. J. Brill). New York: Harper & Brothers Publishing Company.

Bhagavad-Gita: English & Sanskrit. (1984). Translated by Winthrop Sergeant (Rev. ed.). Albany: State University of New York Press.

Bible, English: Authorized. (1903). The English Bible translated out of the original tongues by the commandment of King James the First (anno) 1611. London: D. Nutt Publishing Company.

Bible: English: Revised standard. (1952). The Holy Bible: Revised standard version containing the Old and New Testaments, translated from the original tongues; being the version set forth A. D. 1901; compared with the most ancient authorities and revised A. D. 1952. New York: T. Nelson Publishing Company.

Blavatsky, H. P. (1976). Isis unveiled: A master key to the mysteries of ancient and modern science and theology. Pasadena, California: Theosophical University Press.

Bucke, R. M. (1901). Cosmic consciousness: A study in the evolution of the human mind. New York: E. P. Dutton and Company, Inc.

Claiborne, R. (1977). The birth of writing. Alexandria, VA.: Time-Life Books.

Clodd, E. (1920). The story of the alphabet. New York: D. Appleton and Company.

Crum, W. E. (1962). Coptic dictionary. New York: Oxford University Press, Incorporated.

Diringer, D. (1968). The alphabet: A key to the history of mankind. 3rd Edition completely revised with the assistance of Reinhold Regensburger. New York: Funk & Wagnalls.

Dwight, T., Stoddard, R. H., Marsh, A. R., Van Dyke, P., & Bergh, A. E. (1900). The sacred books of the east. With critical and biographical sketches by Epiphanius Wilson, A.M., Revised edition. Fifth Ave, New York: The Colonial Press.

Hall, M. P. (1937, 1965). Freemasonry of the ancient Egyptians: To which is added an interpretation of the Crata Repoa initiation rite. Los Angeles, California: The Philosophical Research Society, Inc.

Joses (Barnabas) (70 A.D.). The gospel of Barnabas. Edited and Translated From the Imperial Library at Vienna (1907), by Lonsdale and Laura Ragg. Oxford, England: Oxford University Press. (Republished Brooklyn, New York: A & B Books Publishers)

Lord, G. D., Markham, P., Markham, R. H., Merrill, R., & White, C. S. J. (1990). Joseph Campbell: Transformation of myth through time. Orlando, Florida: Harcourt Brace Jovanovich, Publishers.

Mignolo, W. (1995). The darker side of the renaissance: Literacy, territoriality, and colonization. Ann Arbor, Michigan: University of Michigan Press.

Noah, M. (1988). The book of Jasher. Sefer Ha-Yasher, or the Book of Jasher: Referred to in

Joshua and Second Samuel and faithfully translated (1840) from the original Hebrew into English. Thousand Oaks, California, U. S. A.: Artisan Sales.

Shakir, M. H. (1990). <u>The Qur'an</u> (sixth U. S. edition).. Elmhurst, New York: Tahrike Tarsile Qur'an, Inc.

<u>The holy bible: Containing the old and new testaments: Revised standard version: Catholic edition</u>. (1966). Translated from the original tongues being the version set forth A. D. 1611, Old and New Testaments Revised A. D. 1881-1885 and A. D. 1901 (Apocrypha Revised A. D. 1894) compared with the most ancient authorities and revised A. D. 1952 (Apocrypha Revised A. D. 1957). Toronto; Camden, N. J.; London: Thomas Nelson & Sons.

www.ingramcontent.com/pod-product-compliance
Lightning Source LLC
Chambersburg PA
CBHW081331090426
42737CB00017B/3091